BEING A
WISE WOMAN
in a
WILD WORLD

To Barbara ~
All her paths
are peace...
Robin
Chaddock

Robin Chaddock

HARVEST HOUSE PUBLISHERS

EUGENE, OREGON

BEING A WISE WOMAN IN A WILD WORLD
Copyright © 2000/2004 by Robin Chaddock
Published by Harvest House Publishers
Eugene, Oregon 97402
www.harvesthousepublishers.com

Library of Congress Cataloging-in-Publication Data

Chaddock, Robin.
  Being a wise woman in a wild world / Robin Chaddock. Formerly The Proverbial Woman (Winepress, 2000).
    p. cm.
  Includes bibliographical references.
  ISBN 0-7369-1432-3 (pbk.)
    1. Christian women—Religious life. 2. Christian women—Conduct of life. 3. Wisdom. I. Title.
  BV4527.C4 2004
  248.8'43—dc22   2004002118

Lovingly dedicated to Almighty God,
who allowed me this voice in the conversation.

And to my beloved husband, David,
who encourages me to take the time and space to use that voice.

Acknowledgments

I am indebted to beautiful women who took time to dialogue with me and give me input on wisdom. Thank you to Kathy Alderson, Karen Anders, Susan Day, Linda Forler, Jill Funk, Laura Giles, Becky Hagarty, Debbie Harris, Amy Johnston, Jean Knutsen, Karen Lang, Gaye Lindfors, Michele Reel, Denise Rounds, Libby Sandstrom, and Cheree Williams. They are truly a council of wise advisors. To say I couldn't have done it without them is a remarkable understatement.

My heartfelt thanks to the wise and wonderful women of Second Presbyterian Church in Indianapolis, Indiana. They participated in the study groups that helped shape this book and discussion guide. Each woman is so unique, so devoted, and such a treasure. Thank you, ladies!

I am especially grateful to Brenda Clapp who allowed me to use her poem in Chapter 7. Brenda is a highly real, highly wise woman who always speaks from her heart.

CONTENTS

THE
WISDOM PURSUIT

There I stood in the grocery check-out line, mindlessly staring off into space. My daughter, Madison, who was seven at the time, was with me. She was just learning to read. What reading material appears at eye level for a child her age at the check-out counter? *Magazines!*

My mind whipped back to attention when I started hearing her work out the words on the covers and realized what she was reading. She was finding out how to drive a man wild, how to lose 10 pounds fast, how to make her home a showplace, how to have exceptional children, and how to use office gossip to her advantage! And those were just the mild magazines. Thank goodness she hadn't ventured into the sensationalized material!

My seven-year-old was learning how to be a "wise" woman from the covers of popular magazines. But what kind of wisdom was she being taught, and what was it based on?

What in the World Is Going On?

We live in a world where the media, conveniences, political correctness, and fractured relationships play havoc with our sense of balance and the centeredness we need to function as wise women…

The Media

Glamour magazines tell us we must be physically gorgeous to be noticed. Then, once we are noticed, to get and keep a man we must be alluring sexual experts, ready to engage at the drop of a hat. Homemaking magazines taunt us with remarkable entrees and delectable desserts that we should be serving not only to our guests but to our families as well. Regional magazines tempt us with weekend destinations that we should have enough money to go to, not to mention a smoothly running household that can absorb a weekend away into the schedule. The decorating magazines—let's don't even get started on those.

Our wild world inhabits our living rooms in living color at the click of a button. Television, which is such a central part of American life, brings three very unsettling types of images into our lives—images we may embrace as true if we aren't grounded in wisdom.

First the sitcoms and soap operas present sexually loaded, conflict-laden relationships as the norm. In friendships, family, and romance, TV portrays unhealthy patterns of communication and involvement.

Second, the "reality" shows that are so popular are actually anything but reality. These shows imply that high drama, major plastic surgery, having our choice of many suitors at once, voting people out of all kinds of situations, and clawing to the top of the corporate ladder are everyday occurrences that will solve the majority, if not all, of our problems. Most of these shows focus on wealth, beauty, and other types of success as defined by our current culture's standards. These reality shows are rarely reality for most of us.

Third, exposure to news and political shows scare us silly. With emphasis on bad news, tragic conditions, highly conflicted situations, death, and dysfunctional relationships, we live in the uneasy state of never really feeling safe or secure.

The backbone of media is advertising making its living convincing us that we are inadequate and offering all kinds of material pacifiers and self-enhancing services to keep our growing sense of inferiority at bay. We believe more possessions and activities will fill the gaps. Never measuring up leads to over-consumption. We always want more of everything—more money, bigger houses, smarter kids, and more activities. We not only want more, we also want "different" and "novel" on a regular basis.

The crown jewel of the media, the internet, underscores all of these contributions to our wild world as it brings everything—good and bad—into our homes quickly, abundantly, and without boundaries.

Convenience

Technological advances that have added so many conveniences to our lives have also increased the choices we can make. Because of our time-saving devices, we are now able to engage in more discretionary activities. The sheer number of choices we face each day can be numbing. My friend Libby says, "There are so many choices that never existed before, each vying for our attention, that we end up running in circles trying to do everything all the time."

The reality of too many choices makes the world wild for us because we feel we ought to do everything. With so many opportunities to say yes to joining, participating, or volunteering, we feel guilty or left out when we say no. The result is living in the world of overscheduled calendars and 24-hour days that simply aren't enough.

Slippery Values

Our culture also tries to convince us to look the other way when it comes to objectionable or inappropriate behavior. Not wanting to make waves or cause a fuss in the office, school, or extended family keeps us from stating true, godly values of decency, health, and moral wholeness. We witness the questionable behavior of others that doesn't get confronted and figure maybe we're too rigid...or that crime might indeed pay.

Sometimes we feel powerless in the face of the immense evidence that people are making bad choices, striking unethical deals, embracing self-indulgent lifestyles, and laying strength of character and human dignity aside. We may also simply be overwhelmed and exhausted by the life we're trying to lead to worry much about the trouble others are causing or getting into.

"Everybody is doing it" is just as compelling an excuse for adults as it is for teenagers when we are feeling left out or strange because of our beliefs. We get tired of swimming upstream against the flow of immorality.

Fractured Relationships

Some relationships are broken by choice, some relationships are splintered by circumstance. In our chaotic world we move more often, change jobs more often, are separated from our families more often, and have more choices for relationships than ever before. These constant changes make us an individualistic society, where the needs and accomplishments of the individual are more important than the health and needs of the community. We are in danger of believing the bumper sticker that says, "It's all about me," to the detriment of significant, long-lasting, and healthy relationships.

Our cultural belief that "if I'm not happy, I'll just move on" has pervaded families, friendships, and marriages. The 50-percent divorce rate is holding steady—among non-Christians *and* Christians. Sociologists claim that one child in every ten will see his or her parents divorce, experience the remarriage of the parent he or she lives with, and go through their parents' second divorce—all before they turn 16. Choices can indeed fracture relationships.

Even if a family isn't splintered by divorce, a constant barrage of sports practices, volunteer commitments, school functions, art lessons, career responsibilities, and social obligations can crack the family structure, leaving members lonely and isolated from each other. With the rise in home-based technology, four people can be in four different rooms engaged in four different television shows or computer games. Simply living at the pace many of us live can cause family relationships and friendships to fall by the wayside.

We live in a crazy society that has turned day into night and night into day.

We live in a crazy society that has turned day into night and night into day—and no one really knows what the hour is. Cutting to the heart of the matter, my friend Jean, known for her precision and insightfulness, says, "The world is so wild because we have let it become distracting and complex. When we slip off the simple centeredness in God, many things can grab hold of our attention and sap our energies."

The Port

In the midst of false gods, choice chaos, slippery values, murky morality, and ever-shifting standards for relationships, God's wisdom throughout scripture brings the refreshing clarity of a fresh spring breeze sweeping through a dark, dank attic. The essential book of wisdom, Proverbs, is full of short and sweet reminders that fundamentally say, "Do this and live, don't do it and die." Proverbs wisdom stands as a port in the storm-tossed sea of our wild world.

Beckoning from Proverbs is a beautiful and compelling character, Lady Wisdom. She calls to all as she illustrates the difference between life and death, foolishness and wisdom, loyalty and faithlessness. Listening deeply and applying her principles to everyday life brings clearheadedness, vitality, and the knowledge that we don't have to be enslaved to the foolishness of this wild world. There is a better way. Lady Wisdom extends her hand to the sinking and the searching, to the troubled and the lost.

A second compelling woman in the book of Proverbs is found in the very last chapter, Proverbs 31. She is the embodiment of all the wisdom traits we find in wisdom literature. She has been held up for years as a model for Christian womanhood—at times inspiring, at times intimidating—and it's time to make peace with her once and for all. Her story illustrates the ideal, the model of a woman who embraces the wisdom and energy available from God. I like to call her the "Original Wise Woman." She is not put in scripture for us to compare ourselves to her seeming ability to do it all and do it well. She is the proof that godly *characteristics* and *attitudes*—not credentials and accomplishments—identify a wise woman.

As we'll soon see, the startling truth is that the Original Wise Woman in a wild world—the woman of Proverbs 31—is you! You have the same qualities she has—you just have to uncover the unique ways they manifest in you as you grow in the love of God and the power of the Holy Spirit.

The Original Wise Woman was obviously married with children. But today's woman holds any and many stations in life. You may be married, single, divorced. You may be a single mother, a career woman, or a domestic administrator. It doesn't matter if you have a family living in the same home as you do, or if your family is the family of faith at church. You may live at work, you may live alone, or you may live in a house full of people. Wisdom knows no age boundary, no economic structure, no family configuration, no occupational limit. Wisdom is for everyone.

The Joys of Wisdom

The benefits of pursuing wisdom are three powerful P's: perspective, peace, and passion.

Wisdom brings perspective. John Calvin said there are only two kinds of knowledge worth having: knowledge of God and knowledge of self. Becoming women of wisdom means we decide to strip away the temptations and expectations of the world. We will become more comfortable being who we are, and we'll live each and every day accordingly. We begin to fully embrace God's loving care for us and come to understand the true nature of God's estimate of us as His beloved children. We realize for whom and for what we have been created. As we get to know ourselves better, we get to know God better. As we get to know God better, we get to know ourselves better.

Psalms and Proverbs are packed with references to living the life we were created to live and making the contributions we were meant to make as beloved daughters of God. Proverbs 4:25-27 lays out the simple power of walking in our God-given identity:

> Let your eyes look straight ahead,
>   fix your gaze directly before you.
> Make level paths for your feet
>   and take only ways that are firm.
> Do not swerve to the right or the left;
>   keep your foot from evil.

The only sure way to become and remain a wise woman in a wild world is to follow the paths of wisdom, enabling you to have a deeper understanding of yourself because you have a deeper understanding of God.

Wisdom also brings peace. As we make this wisdom journey together, you will find peace because you will discern what is important and what isn't. You will discover how to use all of your unique resources well, including the very powerful resource of your words. You will uncover the ability to focus on God's ways instead of the ways of this wild world. You will become free to value what God values, instead of focusing on what our culture and society think worthwhile. Of Wisdom it is said, "All her paths are peace" (Proverbs 3:17). The epistle writer, James, tells us that the wisdom that comes from heaven is peaceful and brings peace (James 3:18). When you walk in the ways of Wisdom you will find serenity even in the midst of our wild world because you live your life in honesty and integrity.

Finally, wisdom brings passion for living. When you feel secure, when you are not afraid, when you know that you are supported and undergirded by the strong foundation of living in alignment with God, you reclaim the energy for living that you once spent on worrying, comparing, and paying attention to everyone else's business. Anxiety and depression that come from being scared of living can be eased. The less you are weighed down by those cares, the lighter your spirit can be to live with passion. When you realize in whose hands your life rests and by whose hands your life is truly guided, you can rekindle the zest for adventure in your everyday life as you confidently anticipate what the coming day brings.

Do you want perspective, peace, and passion for living? Do you want to be a wise woman in this chaotic world? That's what *Being a Wise Woman in a Wild World* is all about.

Treasure Hunts and Mining Expeditions

Because such a big part of true and pure wisdom comes from knowing ourselves deeply and honestly, the exciting journey of self-discovery is essential to our growth. To walk this path with God by our side, with the Holy Spirit as a loving, gentle, humorous, and encouraging guide, is an expedition in truth telling and truth knowing that will truly set us free.

Throughout this book you'll discover Treasure Hunts—opportunities to grow in self-awareness. Proverbs 3:14-16 assures us:

> [Wisdom] is more profitable than silver
>   and yields better returns than gold.
> She is more precious than rubies;
>   nothing you desire can compare with her.

Long life is in her right hand;
in her left hand are riches and honor.

The Treasure Hunts will help you evaluate where you are and give you insights into what God is currently doing in you. You will have the chance to uncover the riches of wisdom you already have and see where and how you can uncover more as you grow in your life-giving relationship with the one who loves you deeply.

Each chapter also has a "Going Deeper" section to encourage you to actively "mine" wisdom—to interact with scripture, discover the wisdom in your own life, find out what you want to improve, and grow closer to God as you open yourself more completely to the remarkable gift of wisdom.

Read this book with a friend or a group. I've provided plenty of questions to help you understand and embrace wisdom in your life. They will assist your discovery of all you have in common with other women of wisdom in scripture and in our world.

God bless you as you open yourself to the quest for wisdom and the transformation it will bring to your life, to your family, to your work, to your self-image, and to your relationships. In your pursuit and application of wisdom, you will experience a depth of relationship with God you never thought possible!

1

THE WISDOM
WINGDING

*Wise (adj.); marked by deep understanding, keen discern-
ment, and a capacity for sound judgment.*

WEBSTER'S NEW WORLD DICTIONARY

It was an invitation I couldn't refuse. Under the twinkling
Italian lights on the porch of our favorite restaurant on a balmy
Pasadena New Year's Eve, the man I had been crazy in love with
for more than a year invited me to spend the rest of my life with
him.

A year and a month earlier, he had called to extend an invitation for our first date. We both loved jazz, and he wondered if
I would accompany him to a New Year's Eve jazz party. I had to
decline because I had already accepted an invitation from
another gentleman, but I wanted to kick myself for not being
available! With that first date proposition, I knew my interest
was being returned, and I cut the other fellow loose shortly after
New Year's Day!

What made the invitation on the patio so charming was the
way my dear fiancé started the question: "A year ago, I asked

you to join me for New Year's Eve, and you had already accepted another invitation. Tonight I want to make sure that never happens again."

The Invitation

You, too, are loved. You are deeply loved, passionately loved, and eternally loved. The one who loves you is God Almighty, the Maker of heaven and earth. He came to earth in flesh (as Jesus) to prove to you His love. You are never out of His sight, His care, His grace, or His ability. And this God who loves you so much extends to you a special invitation.

Through His good friend and constant companion Wisdom (Proverbs 8:12,22-23), God issues an invitation that is hand-addressed, scented, and delivered with care in a beautiful envelope. He invites you to experience life fully, enthusiastically, and honestly. He makes the invitation to His party so clear and so exciting that you will never accept anyone else's inferior or imitation invitation again! He loves you and desires your company that much! Many times I have heard women say, "I just wish God would write something on the wall or in the sky so I can understand the way to go." Becoming a wise woman in a wild world will set you on the trail of understanding that promises a level path and firm footing (Proverbs 4:26).

Let's take a look at this invitation, the hostess, and the benefits of attending the Wisdom Wingding!

When you send an invitation you prepare for your guests. Lady Wisdom is no exception. Proverbs 9:1-6 tells us:

> Wisdom has built her house; she has hewn out its seven pillars. She has prepared her meat and mixed her wine; she has also set her table. She has sent out her maids, and she calls from the highest point of the city. "Let all who are simple come in here!" she says to those who lack judgment. "Come, eat my food and drink the wine I have

mixed. Leave your simple ways and you will live; walk in the way of understanding."

When you accept Wisdom's invitation, you start on the path of deep understanding and clarified insight. As a woman of wisdom, your life is blessed with at least five party favors when you attend this lifelong event.

Why Should You Come to the Party?

The very first reason to come to the party is that Wisdom is a sure and reliable guide.

I live in the Midwest. Snow and sleet are not strangers to any of us here. That does not, however, mean we like or feel comfortable with them. One Thursday in February, after speaking at my college alma mater to a group of women about their forever identity as God's daughters, I hopped into my van and started my hour-long trek home. A light rain started to fall.

As I traveled south on the main freeway, the light rain quickly turned to heavy rain, then to slushy snow accompanied by gusting winds. It also got dark. I was soon aware that my hands and the steering wheel had become fused together as I struggled to keep my van on the road, especially after each semitrailer rushed by, pelting my van with muck, ice, and slop. My shoulders were hunched up around my ears, and I was scared.

As each truck swooshed by, I thought, "I have just had a wonderful time delivering a very important message in a place that is so meaningful to me—and now it's the last thing I'll ever do! I'll never see my sweet husband or my two wonderful children again" (near death brings out the drama in all of us!). Then my eyes locked onto my salvation.

I discovered what many people already know. Or maybe at the moment it made so much sense to me that I saw it again for the first time. The white line by the side of the road shone as the lifeline by which I could keep my bearings and know I was going to be all right. I kept that guide in sight. My hands relaxed, my shoulders dropped, and I made it home in one wet, cold, sloppy piece.

Wisdom is our guide, our escort, our helmsman through the stormy, muck-slinging days. She is also our advisor and companion through fair weather times. Wisdom is as obvious and available as the white line by the side of the road; she is as constant as that painted beacon that keeps us all from careening down bumpy, treacherous roads.

All who attend the Wisdom Wingding receive a luscious goody bag. Proverbs 3:13-18,21-26 sum up the many party favors of answering positively to Lady Wisdom's invitation:

> Blessed is the man who finds wisdom, the man who gains understanding, for she is more profitable than silver and yields better returns than gold. She is more precious than rubies; nothing you desire can compare with her. Long life is in her right hand; in her left hand are riches and honor. Her ways are pleasant ways, and all her paths are peace. She is a tree of life to those who embrace her; those who lay hold of her will be blessed....
>
> My son, preserve sound judgment and discernment, do not let them out of your sight; they will be life for you, an ornament to grace your neck. Then you will go on your way in safety, and your foot will not stumble; when you lie down, you will not be afraid; when you lie down, your sleep will be sweet. Have no fear of sudden disaster or of the ruin that overtakes the wicked, for the LORD will be your confidence and will keep your foot from being snared.

That's a pretty tall order. It's a long list of benefits or excellent returns when you invest your life in the pursuit of wisdom. Let's look at five of these favors in ϵ ~~terms.~~

22

Happiness. Happiness is another term for l many people are chasing how many things arouna us eveiy uay, trying to find happiness? How many possessions, provisions, and prizes are we pursuing on a perpetual basis as we look for that moment when we feel we can exhale and relax because we have finally "made it"? Happiness is readily available to Christians who pursue wisdom because "the fear of the LORD is the beginning of wisdom" (Proverbs 9:10). Fear is reverence, respect, and honor. "Fear of the Lord" means we are struck with awe by God's being, power, capabilities, and character. Fear of the Lord draws us into a mysterious intimacy with the Almighty that effectively blocks our ability to be obsessed with ourselves, our schemes, and our own solutions to our problems. Happiness is a result of being saved from ourselves when we have a full-fledged ambition to seek God's face and embrace His dear friend Wisdom in the process. One definition for the happiness that wisdom brings is: I know who I am, I know who God is, and I don't get the two confused. This represents a lifelong process, to be sure.

Riches, honor, and length of days. Riches and honor are listed in Wisdom's treasure chest, as is a long life. When looking at these benefits, we must always be aware that God's ways are not our ways and His thoughts are not our thoughts (Isaiah 55:8). While we may enjoy riches, honor, and long life offered from a worldly perspective, one of the true benefits of pursuing and grasping Wisdom is the transformation in our thinking and values that comes from honoring God and putting His ways first.

For roughly 39 years of my life, I could think of nothing more desirable than a comfortable home, a modest closet full of clothes, a nice car to drive, understated elegance in my jewelry, and the smug (and fake) humility of being a recognizable and oteworthy person. I did everything I could to make all of this happen. My favorite thing to do was work. My passion was career advancement. More work, more money. Better career, better earning power. Even after my children were born, work was the focal point of my life.

All the while I was becoming more miserable. Caring for the kids kept me from putting all of my energy and ambition into earning money. Having domestic responsibilities hindered me from pursuing riches and honor as I had defined them. No job could make me money fast enough. And on top of all of that, we were going into debt at such a rate that we had to give up our big, custom-built home for a smaller house. As blinded as I was by the god Jesus called Mammon, I did not even realize that "we eventually cannot afford what we most desire—deep relationships. For if 'time is money' and people take time, then the 'opportunity costs of relationships' (the gain that we would earn by doing something else) will be prohibitive and intimate friendships will be few. 'Spending' time with friends is costly; we could 'invest' it better elsewhere."[1]

Have you ever read the Bible and seen something but were somehow blinded to how much it applied to you? That's exactly where I was as I read and knew of James' warning, "For where you have envy and selfish ambition, there you find disorder and every evil practice" (James 3:16). Being unwise often means we are sightless to how out of balance and unaligned our own lives are. That's certainly where I was.

I am grateful every day for God's grace and mercy. He allowed me to come to the end of myself, to grow up, and to come to maturity in Him day by day, which helped me see the beauty and riches in my life as it was. Thankfully, God didn't have to bring me any tragedies to jolt me into submission. In His persistence and goodness, He introduced me to His friend Wisdom and suggested I get to know her intimately and permanently.

Because of Wisdom's friendship, I have discovered kids are not a condiment in life—something you throw on top of everything else when it is convenient. To smell your children's hair, to hear them giggle, to break up a fight, to speak words of instruction every day only to hear them repeated to younger siblings at a later time are some of the richest experiences available. To smile at your beloved spouse across the room and know that there is deep affection between you, to share openly and honestly with your life partner on a regular basis, to have him speak kind words of you in public are honors saved only for those who are patient, watchful, and wise. Whether you're married or single, long life is measured by the laughter around a simple meal with good friends. Length of days is assessed by the evenings you can lay your head on your pillow knowing that your very life has meant something to God that day. Those are the riches and honor of wisdom. That is the length of days that reverence for God will put into your life.

Peace and pleasantness. One of our deepest longings is for peace of mind. So why are we constantly trading pleasant ways for selfish ways? Harmony for haughtiness? Orderliness for orneriness? Tranquility for truckloads of stuff? Wisdom promises peace and pleasantness. Perhaps this lacks the excitement and danger that our adrenaline-addicted society demands on a daily basis to stay stimulated and "feel" alive. The difference between the two lifestyles is the contrast between being constantly buzzed then abandoned by caffeine and being cleansed and renewed by fresh spring water. The first one seems to be the way to being fully alive, but it only provides diminishing returns as a person is catapulted down the spiral of addiction and increasing need. The second provides a cool, thirst-quenching refreshment that revitalizes the body and provides a sense of comfort.

Perhaps the most tangible and necessary way wisdom provides peace is through a good night's sleep (Proverbs 3:24). As wise women in a wild world, we sleep better because our integrity, our honesty, and our love—and the rewards of that love—will move us through our days into nights that have no regrets.

How many times have you gone to bed saying, "I wish I hadn't said that today"? How many times have you been awakened with a start in the middle of the night thinking, "Oh, how am I going to solve this problem?" How many times have you risen early, but felt there wasn't anything in particular to rise early for? As we learn from Wisdom how to speak, act, and respond as women of wisdom, we will lay our heads on our pillows at night able to rest securely in God's arms. We will sleep soundly and awake refreshed in the morning, ready to move out into the new day with purpose and peace, taking the Master's hand for the next adventure.

No fear. What are you afraid of? Financial hardship? A child straying? Not being important or recognized? Getting to the end of life and wondering what just happened? Not having enough? An affair? Wisdom promises that when we walk in step with her, we will have nothing to fear. This does not mean we may not fall on hard times. Her promise is we will not have *cause* to fear. Being a wise woman in a wild world means we know who we are in God's world and in God's heart. It means we tend our relationships to make them strong and healthy. Being a woman of wisdom means we each understand our essential call—who we are in Christ and what His particular purpose for our lives is—and live that call with passion. It means we have life's priorities in proper order. It also means we are so in tune with all of the needs in our self and in others and the resources to meet those needs that we have no time for idle fretting!

Sure feet. One summer, during the four years I was director of youth ministries at my church, I took the kids to a Young Life camp in Colorado. Young Life camps are not for the fainthearted! Every day is packed with new adventures.

One day it was my cabin's turn to take on the challenge of the ropes course. A ropes course is a series of logs, bridges, and swings a fair number of feet off the ground. Although participants are on a belay line to save them from hurting the ground should they lose their footing, it is still a frightening experience for many.

I was one of the many. The first test of the ropes course was to walk one foot in front of the other up a log that angled from the ground to a spot about 20 feet off the ground where the actual course began. From there, I was going to walk across another 20-foot log until I reached the "safety" of the next task, the rope bridge. Being a counselor, I had to do this. Staying securely on the ground was not an option for one in leadership!

Wisdom promises us that our feet, our steps, our path will be steady and secure.

My knees shook. I clenched the belay line with my hands as if it was going to help steady my trembling body. I wanted to cry, but could show no fear. My mind was screaming out, "Don't do this to me! Have you no sense?"

I made it up the inclined log and then across the suspended log. It took a long time, but I did it. Every step was accompanied by the sure conviction that my wobbly legs were going to give out, and I was going to get hurt. But by the grace of God, I made it.

What makes you go weak in the knees? Walking into a room full of strangers or friends? Heights? Balancing the checkbook? Thinking about facing one more day of dirty diapers or endless paperwork? Confrontation with your family? The thought of tending a dying child or parent?

Wisdom promises us that our feet, our steps, our path will be steady and secure as we become better friends with this gift of God (Proverbs 3:26). Because reverence for the Lord is the beginning of wisdom, our sights are taken off our feet and set on the Author and Finisher of our faith (Hebrews 12:2). Our eyes are taken off the raging seas around us and fixed on the hand and face of the one who controls everything (Mark 4:35-41).

"PARTY FAVOR" TREASURE HUNT

How much do you currently enjoy the five party favors given to wise women in our wild world? Use the following scale in responding to each statement:

5=always   4=often   3=sometimes   2=rarely   1=never

_____ 1. I am happy because I know who I am, I know who God is, and I don't get the two confused.

_____ 2. I understand and embrace riches, honor, and length of days from God's perspective rather than from the world's perspective.

_____ 3. I have peace and pleasantness in my life.

_____ 4. I am confident of the days to come, knowing that my life is in order and God is my ultimate protection and provision.

_____ 5. My path is steady, and I walk securely.

The higher your score, the more you are enjoying the benefits of being a wise woman. Which party favors are you lacking? What might you need to concentrate on for them to become more abundant in your life? Which party favors are you enjoying to the fullest? How can you share them with others around you in a way that invites them to enjoy wisdom as well?

The Original Wise Woman

She has been hated; she has been dismissed. She has been the source of finger wagging by men and chagrin among women at whom those fingers were wagged. One woman at a retreat I led called her "that psycho Proverbs woman!" She is the woman described by King Lemuel's mother in the thirty-first chapter of the book of Proverbs.

When I first met her, I didn't know whether to kick her or kiss her. Should I bless her because she gives some wonderful guidelines? Or should I curse her because she is an impossible standard? As author Melissa Jansen says, "When I see all the areas in which this woman displays prudent living, I realize I have two choices. The first is to cut Proverbs 31 out of my husband's Bible so he doesn't get any ideas. The second is to be challenged enough to change."[2]

Well, as is the wise thing to do when you do not know much about certain people—before you decide to write them off—you should get to know them at least a little. After all, we are to do to others what we want them to do to us (Matthew 7:12)! So I started snooping around to see what this Proverbs woman is all about.

First I carefully read Proverbs 31:10-31:

> A wife of noble character who can find? She is worth far more than rubies. Her husband has full confidence in her and lacks nothing of value. She brings him good, not harm, all the days of her life. She selects wool and flax and works with eager hands. She is like the merchant ships, bringing her food from afar. She gets up while it is still dark; she provides food for her family and portions for her servant girls. She considers a field and buys it; out of her earnings she plants a vineyard. She sets about her work vigorously; her arms are strong for her tasks. She sees that her trading is profitable, and her lamp does not go out at night.
>
> In her hand she holds the distaff and grasps the spindle with her fingers. She opens her arms to the poor and extends her hands to the needy. When it snows, she has no fear for her household; for all of them are clothed in scarlet. She makes coverings for her bed; she is clothed in fine linen and purple. Her husband is respected at the city gate, where he takes his seat among

the elders of the land. She makes linen garments and sells them, and supplies the merchants with sashes.

She is clothed with strength and dignity; she can laugh at the days to come. She speaks with wisdom, and faithful instruction is on her tongue. She watches over the affairs of her household and does not eat the bread of idleness. Her children arise and call her blessed; her husband also, and he praises her: "Many women do noble things, but you surpass them all." Charm is deceptive, and beauty is fleeting; but a woman who fears the LORD is to be praised. Give her the reward she has earned, and let her works bring her praise at the city gate.

Thankfully, there are at least three ideas about this superheroine that make it possible to be in the same room with her.

Composite. Perhaps the king's mother had taken a survey of the best qualities available in Hebrew women at the time. As she penned her advice to her son (imagine being her daughter-in-law!), she drew on all the superlatives she could find. The "Original Wise Woman" may be a composite, much as if we took pictures of individual women doing the most noteworthy things a woman can do and pasted them all together.

She is an amalgam of all the characteristics we see running through biblical wisdom literature. She is wisdom personified, so we can say, "If one person completely embodied all the characteristics of wisdom, this is what she would look like." My friend Libby explained it this way, "I don't feel there is any one woman who has been a model of wisdom to me. My friends each have their own area in which they are wise. Some have wisdom regarding the physical body, some are wise in handling their spiritual needs, some are wise in their financial dealings, and some are wise in their family life. A few of them are wise in several areas."

Poetry. The first letter of each line in this acrostic poem is the successive Hebraic alphabet. This woman has so many wonderful features because there were 22 letters in the Hebrew alphabet! If we were to write the same poem today, our charged-up woman of wisdom would have 26 remarkable characteristics.

Lifetime Overview. Author Annie Chapman suggests, "Proverbs 31 is a list of lifetime accomplishments, rather than a log of a particular day. When I look at Proverbs 31 as a lifetime resumé of a mature woman, it gives me hope."[3] This view suggests that this litany of notable qualities is a description of a woman who is past middle age, who has had a long time to accomplish many things and develop many skills. This passage isn't a page or even a week from her day planner book or PDA! It might be the kind of speech given at a retirement dinner or at an eightieth birthday banquet. Or it might be the kind of tribute my friend Karen wrote for her mother, who died suddenly in November 2003:

> When you asked me, "Who has been a model to you of wise womanhood," the first woman I think of is my mother, Patricia Anderson. She was 68 years young when she passed away recently, and far many years wiser than that. She was my best friend, my confidant, and my mentor.
>
> As I reflect back on her life, I see a wise woman who set many good examples for those lives she touched. She was the nucleus of our family, the glue that held us together. She was a woman of faith. She was loving and nurturing; kind and compassionate; comforting and supportive.
>
> Once you had her love, it was never-ending. Her faith in you unfailing, no matter what. You had her support, comfort, and compassion in whatever your endeavors. She was there to praise you and celebrate your accomplishments and victories. If you failed at

something, she was there with her love and guidance to help you pick up the pieces and move forward. She let you know how proud of you she was under both circumstances.

She gave unselfishly of her time and knowledge. She bought and delivered supplies to the local humane society, volunteered her time at church or the community women's club, cared for and comforted sick friends, taught people to crochet or cross-stitch, and knitted and crocheted blankets for the local nursing home. She shared her many talents and gifts with others.

She had a wonderful sense of humor, was comfortable with herself, and was a gracious host. People wanted to be around her whether it be at a weekly gathering with her lady friend, at a club meeting, or at the theatre. Her home was always open to friends and family—a vacation spot for travelers and a gathering spot for friends to share a festive meal and a fun-filled evening together.

She was the kind of person who you were proud to call your friend. She spoke to you honestly and wasn't a gossip. If she made a promise to you, she kept it. She would send friend and family handwritten postcards, notes, and greeting cards on a regular basis just to say "I'm thinking of you" or "I love you" or to offer encouragement or comfort. Little surprises would come in the mail that were handmade by her just to let you know she was thinking of you and that she cared.

A friend once told me that I was the type of person who always tried to see the good in everyone. That was a gift from my mother. She was the same way, and I try my best to live by her example.

I only hope that I can be half the wise woman in my lifetime that she was in hers. I mourn her loss with my whole being. I will love her eternally and treasure the moment I get to see her again in heaven.

The best thing that could happen to any of us in this life is for someone to feel about us what Karen expresses for her mother.

Any of these three views—composite, poetry, lifetime overview—gives hope to the young, the harried, and the frustrated. Our Proverbs 31 friend is a woman just like any of us who has grasped the one ingredient necessary to make her a distinguished woman and an example for the rest of us: "A woman who fears the LORD is to be praised" (Proverbs 31:30).

When we look at her and growl, it reminds me of my dog, Maggie, looking at her reflection in a mirror while she plays with a chew toy. Maggie doesn't know she is actually looking at herself. She thinks there is another dog trying to take something precious away from her. Maggie's defensiveness comes from the fact that she is focused on herself and the fear that she is going to lose something in a struggle. When we roll our eyes, groan, or make that disdainful sniffing sound at the mention of this Proverbs woman, we are doing so because we have our eyes on ourselves, and we are growling at our own reflection!

If you are intimidated or disgusted by this Original Wise Woman, if you are tempted, like my friend Melissa, to rip that passage out of your Bible, reexamine what you focus on in creation. You may be glued to the creature and not the Creator. Instead of dismissing this important passage of Scripture because you feel you cannot measure up, embrace this passage as a picture of the possibilities and more when you seek God's face and Wisdom's friendship.

The most important thing to remember is this: The Wise Woman of Proverbs 31 was not honored by God because she was a superwoman. She was a super woman because she honored God.

How Do You Become a Wise Woman in a Wild World?

If you want all the benefits discussed in this chapter so far, plus many more, become a woman of wisdom! You will have six distinguishing features coloring your life with satisfaction, abundance, peace, and honor. The rest of this book will unpack these traits, show you how to make them your own, and give real-life examples of women who have been changed for God's glory as they decided to walk hand in hand with an eternal and trusted friend—Wisdom.

You are a wise woman in a wild world when you—

1. *Let God draw you to Himself.* The end of the quest is also the beginning: "The fear of the LORD is the beginning of Wisdom" (Proverbs 9:10). We will lay the foundation for becoming a woman of wisdom. How do we get started? What do we need to do in actual step-by-step instructions to get into the proper relationship with God that allows wisdom to infiltrate and transform our lives?

2. *Let God work through you.* We will look at the zeal you will gain for life when you grasp and understand the essential call for which you have been created. Your days and years will be energized as you learn to say no to the temptations that cloud your understanding of the essence of God's purpose for your life. Your vision will gain clarity and your behavior will resemble more a steady stream than a raging rapid. A wise woman is very sure of her call and capabilities. She lives her life with noticeable passion and effectiveness.

3. *Let God communicate through you.* For anyone who has ever said, "I should have said..." or "I wish I hadn't said..." we will look at the top-ten ways you can be a woman of wise speech. If you have ever bemoaned, "I should have listened when..." we will explore how to discern the wise advisor from the fool. We'll unpack scriptural passages that give us unmistakable advice for speaking and listening.

4. *Let God minister through you.* As far as she is able, a wise woman "opens her arms to the poor and extends her hands to the needy" (Proverbs 31:20). She not only ministers directly to those in obvious need, she acts as a support to those closest to her, enabling them to carry on their missions in the community. Her service flows naturally in all she does and all she is.

5. *Let God laugh through you.* A wise woman is a terrific steward. She takes care of herself, her family, and her community. She watches over all God has given her. Because she is so faithful, she makes an impact wherever she goes, and she can "laugh at the days to come" (Proverbs 31:25).This laughter signals a light heart as she enters each day knowing all is ultimately well. She looks ahead, invests wisely by counting the cost, cares for the details, and hums her way through life, confident that the cold winds may blow yet she and those she loves will be protected.

6. *Let God love through you.* Whatever your family configuration, you are part of a birth family and a global family. We will look at four ways in particular to be the gift to others that God created you to be.

Your RSVP

If you are like most women, the first envelopes you open when you shuffle through the daily mail are the envelopes that have been hand-addressed, have a return address from someone you know and love, perhaps have been scented, and are packaged in beautiful papers that set them apart from the rest.

The invitation to the Wisdom Wingding has been sent. You have opened the envelope. You may choose to throw the invitation on the pile of unheeded, unanswered mail, but the invitation has been extended just the same. If you choose not to respond positively, please examine your reason. Is it akin to the excuses given by the guests specially invited to the Great Banquet in Luke 14:15-24? Are you too busy to pursue wisdom? Are you afraid you won't know anyone at the party? Are you just not interested in having your life transformed into the beauty God intended for you? Do you simply prefer to design your own parties for one?

I responded to the invitation of my soon-to-be husband under those sparkling lights with a resounding, "Yes!" There was no hesitation, no deliberation! I certainly could not foresee everything the future would hold for us, but I knew he was the one I wanted to go with into that future. I said yes to the invitation, and I've been saying yes to the marriage every day since.

RSVP positively to this Wisdom Wingding invitation! Nurture your budding desire to become a wise woman in a wild world, and walk through the door to the most exciting, lifelong party you'll ever attend!

GOING DEEPER

Warm-up: Our responses to the many invitations we receive, large and small, shape our character and define our beliefs. What we say yes and no to gives us a window to understand our nature and the opportunity to shape that nature in partnership with the Holy Spirit to conform to the image of God. Accepting or declining invitations weaves the fabric of our lives. Are you going to accept Wisdom's invitation?

1. Read Proverbs 8:1-12,32-36; 9:1-6. What does Wisdom offer her guests? What makes her invitation attractive? Is this invitation compelling to you? Why or why not?

2. Read Proverbs 7:10-27; 9:13-18. What does the harlot offer her guests? What makes her invitation attractive? Is this invitation compelling to you? Why or why not?

3. It has been observed that the invitation of the harlot seems more enticing, more flashy, more glamorous than Wisdom's invitation. What modern examples can you see around you of the invitations issued by both these forces?

4. Read Proverbs 8:22-31. How long has Wisdom been at God's side? What is Wisdom's response toward human beings?

5. When have you known that someone was delighted in you, that he or she thought you were something special? How did that person's opinion of you affect your relationship?

6. How does knowing that Wisdom is God's intimate companion and is delighted in you impact your pursuit of wisdom?

7. Read the following passages of Scripture. In your own words, give each of the benefits a name.

   1. Proverbs 3:13—
   2. Proverbs 3:2,16a—
   3. Proverbs 3:17; 3:24—
   4. Proverbs 3:6,23; 4:25-26—
   5. Proverbs 1:33; 3:26—
   6. Proverbs 3:8,18a—
   7. Proverbs 3:16b—

8. Review the list and thoughtfully describe what each of these benefits would look like in your life. Which are the most appealing to you at this point in your life? Why?

9. Write the letters of our alphabet down the side of a page. Then use the letters to list character traits, skills, interests, and passions that you possess. Congratulations! You've just written Proverbs 31 about yourself.

10. Write out the script you would like someone to read in a speech that honors you later in your life.

11. Read Psalm 111:10. This biblical fear can be defined this way: I know who I am and I know who God is, and I don't get the two confused. What is your definition of this kind of "fear"? What does it mean to you to fear the Lord?

Assignment for this week: Be aware of billboards, magazine covers, television and radio ads. What kinds of invitations are they sending you?

2

THE BOTTOM LINE

If you don't know what you're doing, pray to the Father. He loves to help. You'll get his help and won't be condescended to when you ask for it.

JAMES 1:5 MSG

The life of the spirit, by integrating us in the real order established by God, puts us in the fullest possible contact with reality—not as we imagine it, but as it really is.

THOMAS MERTON

Accepting the invitation and stepping into the Wisdom party begs the very first question—How do we get started? Yes, we want to have more peace and purpose in our lives! Yes, we want to speak, act, think, and relate more wisely! Yes, we want to walk hand-in-hand with Wisdom and her creator, God Almighty! But how do we do it?

Our quest is outlined by one very short half-verse in the book of Psalms: "The fear of the LORD is the beginning of wisdom" (111:10). This fear is one of awe, of appreciating the mighty distinction between God and us, and realizing that this

God is also living in us. Through the gift of the Holy Spirit, God dwells in each of us. Because we are created in God's image, God shines through us. But we must never forget that we are creatures, not Creator. We are beloved, not the Lover. God is present in all that we see, but all that we see does not total God. There is much more to Him. We can meditate, study, pray, discuss, and ponder God our whole lives and only scratch the surface of His being. Through His presence in our joys and anguish, we have a veiled sense of the immeasurable depth of God's love, wisdom, and might.

A Tale of Two Ladies

To more fully appreciate the assertion that proper relating to God is the beginning of wisdom, we can look at the contrast between two prominent women in the Old Testament. Both had very similar characteristics and ambitions. The stark difference is in their foundation, in the tilt of their hearts.

One name in the Old Testament is synonymous with evil, treachery, greed, and vanity. Fear reigns in the heart today when a woman is nicknamed Jezebel! The book of 2 Kings tells of her devotion to her husband's career. After all, as long as Ahab was king, Jezebel was, of course, queen. She possessed incredible people-management skills, evidenced by the huge stable of Baal prophets she directed. She ran a huge household, serving dinner to as many as 850 people in one sitting. She was beautiful, smart, and goal-oriented. She shared many qualities with the "Original Wise Woman."

But Jezebel lacked one critical leaning. She did not honor or revere the Lord. She killed God's prophets and slandered His kings. She put her stock in her looks, her husband's position, the massive entourage she had surrounded herself with, and her ability to make people do exactly what she wanted.

Just before her demise, reported in 2 Kings 9:30-37, she painted her eyes and arranged her hair. She taunted Jehu, God's appointed king, as he came into the city. She yelled at him out an upper-story window, and he replied by instructing two or three men inside to push her through. The telling of her death is rather gruesome in the details, but one aspect is quite note-worthy. After Jehu had eaten a meal and taken drink, he directed Jezebel be buried for, after all, "she was a king's daughter" (verse 34). When the people who were to bury her went outside to gather her body, "they found nothing except her skull, her feet and her hands" (verse 35). There was nothing left of the woman! Because of her evil, the Lord ordained that she could not be found by anyone forever after: "This is the word of the LORD that he spoke through his servant Elijah the Tishbite: On the plot of ground at Jezreel dogs will devour Jezebel's flesh. Jezebel's body will be like refuse on the ground in the plot at Jezreel, so that no one will be able to say, 'This is Jezebel'" (verses 36-37). After all of her conquests, commands, cosmetics, and career moves, there was not a thing left of her life. Because of her faulty grounding, her life and legacy meant absolutely nothing.

"Charm is deceptive, and beauty is fleeting; but a woman who fears the LORD is to be praised" (Proverbs 31:30). The wise woman of Proverbs 31 had her focus set on pleasing God. She put aside worldly ambitions and expectations. She decided not to believe the fashion magazines and the gossip shows. She kept her sights on the one who made her, loved her, and intimately guided the steps of her day. Because of this, her legacy lived on, her name was exalted in the city gates, and her family spoke of her for years to come. Her life meant something. Her work car-ried on. Her hands are also noted in this famous passage. They extend to the poor and the needy (verse 20) and work willingly, using her gifts and talents to provide for the community and her family (verses 13,19).

Graciously, the book of Proverbs gives us deeper insight into the pursuit and capture of wisdom for our lives. In two well-defined steps, God and His companion Wisdom show us how to live in honor, reverence, awe, and fear of the Lord. In one beautiful poetic couplet (Psalm 31:30), we are given the keys to tranquility, passion, and influence.

The Investment in Wisdom

In the world of business and finance, the bottom line refers to the summary of a cost–benefit analysis. After business owners have weighed what they will need to invest, expend, or sacrifice against the probable gains, they look at the bottom line and decide if this will be worth the time, energy, and capital of their company. Proverbs 3:5-6 calls us to the bottom line. If you want to become a woman of wisdom, here is the investment required and the promised return:

> Trust in the LORD with all your heart and lean not on your own understanding; in all your ways acknowledge him, and he will make your paths straight.

Trust in the Lord. What is trust? Trust is sitting down in a chair, believing it will hold you up. It's flipping on a light switch—expecting the light to come on. Trust is entering into the stoplight intersection when you have a green light, figuring that cross traffic is going to respect their red lights. But trust can go even deeper. Dr. William G. Enright, senior minister of Second Presbyterian Church in Indianapolis, says, "Trust is a combination of competence and reliability." With this definition of trust, our faith in God is well-grounded.

God's competence is God's might. God's competence is centered in His wisdom and design. Is God able to handle the situation? Is the Creator of the universe, the God who deeply, passionately, and eternally loves you, capable of understanding and directing your life? Do you truly believe what the angel Gabriel said when speaking to Jesus' mother Mary: "For nothing is impossible with God" (Luke 1:37)?

God's competence is highly revealed in His conversations with Job. After Job has been tested, not only by Satan, but by his well-meaning friends, God takes over and brings Job to a higher level of awareness and awe of the Almighty's work and wonder in the universe and in Job's life.

> Where were you when I laid the earth's foundation? Tell me, if you understand....Have you ever given orders to the morning, or shown the dawn its place?...Have you journeyed to the springs of the sea or walked in the recesses of the deep?...Do you know the laws of the heavens? Can you set up [God's] dominion over the earth? Can you raise your voice to the clouds, and cover yourself with a flood of water? (38:4,12,16,33-34).

The answers to these and many more questions are, of course, sheepish nos. But God does not intend to humiliate Job or us with these questions. He intends to lovingly and accurately turn our perspective so we can again know that He is in control, that He has set everything in motion, and that He is able to guide our lives with passion and precision. God does not seek to indict, but to invite, as He bids us look at the mind- and heart-expanding wonders of His competence.

> By wisdom the LORD laid the earth's foundations,
>   by understanding he set the heavens in place;
> By his knowledge the deeps were divided,
>   and the clouds let drop the dew (Proverbs 3:19-20).

God's reliability is His faithfulness. Moses comforts the people of Israel during a leadership transition when he encourages and promises in Deuteronomy 31:6: "Be strong and courageous. Do not be afraid or terrified because of them, for the LORD your God goes with you; he will never leave you nor forsake you." Does God have a good track record in Scripture and in the everyday lives of contemporary people of faith? Psalm 139:7-10 asks and answers—

> Where can I go from your Spirit? Where can I flee from your presence? If I go up to the heavens, you are there; if I make my bed in the depths, you are there. If I rise on the wings of the dawn, if I settle on the far side of the sea, even there your hand will guide me, your right hand will hold me fast.

Have you ever known God to drop the ball? As Cheri Fuller says, "When I would take a baby step toward God by praying about something, He'd answer, and I'd see a little more of His faithfulness. It was as if He was saying, 'Yes, I'm here. I care. I'm faithful. Keep coming to me'—much as we stretch out our hands to our little ones when they take their first steps."[1]

Why are we afraid to trust God? Because we cannot help humanizing Him. Especially when we are young in faith, we relate to God like we do with other authority figures in our lives. If we have difficulty in trusting God, it may reflect a relationship with a neglectful father, an overprotective mother, an abusive older sibling, or an unpredictable grandparent. Over time, with good nurture and modeling from steady people of faith, those uncertainties and blocks can be overcome. We must often trust God's Word, choosing to set aside the conditioning of our past lives. To move into a deeper place of trust, we need to constantly pray for the transforming work of the Holy Spirit, and then watch for the transformation as it unfolds. In short, we need to remember that God is not those who have hurt us in the past, and those who have hurt us in the past were not acting as true representatives of God.

But what if God intends to take us someplace we don't want to go? When I was a newly blossoming teenager, a missionary couple came to speak at the Sunday evening service of my church. I have no clear memory of what they said, but I have a very clear memory of being scared to death that I was going to have to do what they had done. If I were going to be a real disciple, I would be taken to heinous and scary places to prove my love for God. But this view of faith completely ignores God's great love for me, His deep and passionate love that seeks communion with me. It totally undermines the understanding that God created me for a purpose and that my joy would be complete in the fulfilling of that purpose.

But what if trusting God means I have to give up control? Well, the good news/bad news is that is exactly what it means! An objection to this simply shows an absence of understanding and faith in Scripture and the nature of God's competence and reliability. Seeking to stay in control divorces ourselves from God and denies the truth that God has been and continues to be at work for our benefit to give us a future and a hope (Jeremiah 29:11). The God who loves you deeply, passionately, and eternally is your partner, not your puppet master! What do you want to control that you think you can handle better than God can? What do you want to keep from His view and direction? And why is it in your life anyway, if you want to keep it from God?

The power to come to a deeper trust in God is in the dynamic alliance of you and the Holy Spirit.

Every day the newscasts and the morning paper give us new examples of children who have been abused by someone they love and trust. Increasingly the statistics rise, and we know of more and more children who suffer this indignant injustice. One of the most heartbreaking consequences is their inability to form intimate relationships with others, especially God. The abuse may have even been "religious"—what one therapist calls "spiritual rape," in which the child had religious "truths" forced upon him or her without regard to conversation, questions, or individual temperament. The struggle is then enormous to come to comfort in God's presence, in the silence and warmth of God's care. Such a person may be able to lead a religious life, but true trust and delight in being a child of God, a partner with God, a lover of God is hard to understand, much less experience. The difference between knowing *about* God and *knowing* God is monumental.

Any of these reasons why it is difficult to trust God is worthy of critical and thorough examination. They are real and powerful roadblocks to the many rich returns of wisdom we uncovered in Chapter 1. Do not let these negative circumstances take you prisoner any longer. Realize that it is now time to heal and to take charge of your response to these spiritual obstacles. The power to come to a deeper trust in God is in the dynamic alliance of you and the Holy Spirit.

Lean not on your own understanding. What is understanding? Look in a thesaurus, and it's easy to see the wisdom in giving God control of your heart, vision, and direction. Understanding is intelligence and a view of the big picture. What is our intelligence compared to God's? How does our grasp on the overall big picture of our lives compare to God's view of our lives? Understanding is awareness and discernment. How does our awareness of world and historical events stack up to the overall discernment God has? When we take a good look at these questions and their answers, it becomes almost comical that any of us should lean on our own understanding. It would be funny, except it's sometimes so tragic.

I love the way Debbie states it: "I guess in short it means that things are not always as they appear, and surrendering to the Lord completely is what will keep us going in the right direction. My perception of how things are is not always right. (In fact, my perception is often wrong!) Fighting for control of a situation is an uphill battle that we will more often than not lose."

In all your ways acknowledge Him. To acknowledge means to recognize something or someone for its true essence. It means to take notice of and be grateful. "In all your ways" has at least four applications:

1. *Manner.* In the way you are, recognize and reflect God. In your speech, your dress, your attitudes, let on to others that God is the authority of your life. When people say, "She has a certain manner about her," let that manner or spirit about you declare the presence of the Holy Spirit in your life.

2. *Means.* How do you get things done? In what way do you operate? Do you approach life and situations with hope, honesty, and respect for others? Do you work with integrity? Are you demanding, cooperative, passive, forceful, commanding, inviting? The way you get things done—the means to your ends—needs to confirm your relationship with God. You acknowledge or disavow God in your life as you move through your daily chores and conversations. Do others see you acknowledge God in your ways?

3. *Miles.* Where are you going? In your relationships, your finances, your career, and your acquisitions, do you acknowledge or cherish God? Do you see and appreciate God? Do you reply and respond to God in openness and gratitude? To acknowledge God in your miles means you are aware of the decisions you need to make, and you turn to God for direction. You listen for the still, small voice that says, "This is the way; walk in it" (Isaiah 30:21).

4. *Milieu.* Does your environment tell others that God is walking by your side? Would others know by looking at the magazines on your coffee table, the art on your walls, the trappings of your surroundings that you are in a loving, peace-filled relationship with the Almighty? Are

you living in chaos or order (I didn't say perfect cleanliness!)? Does your atmosphere reflect peace or agitation?

When you acknowledge God in these ways, you open the door for His guidance. You and God partner to let people know who you are and whose you are. The Holy Spirit will also more smoothly and effortlessly flow through and over you to guide and direct your steps, your interactions, and your reflections so that you are walking in wisdom.

God has given us wonderful means to acknowledge His presence, passion, and participation in our lives. It's found in P-R-A-Y.

P—Pause. Stop for a moment and look at the sky. Or drink in the scents and sounds of your favorite season. Savor the taste of your "comfort food." Take time to really hug a friend, hold a child, kiss your beloved. Our five senses are the first five gifts God gave us upon birth. He is constantly showering us with messages of His desire for us to enjoy His world and all the gifts therein. When we honestly take in a truly pleasurable sensory experience, our souls will often sigh, "Ah." That sigh is a prayer of gratitude and an acknowledgment of God's grace and cleverness in creation.

R—Reflect. One of the best ways to reflect is through writing. Anne Broyles ponders,

> We are gifted with a space and time to open ourselves to the Lover of the World. Journaling is a private discipline in which we can reveal ourselves totally. There is no need to carefully consider words or wonder what other people might think of our thoughts. Journal writing is sharing between our true selves and the God of Truth. In journaling, we come to know ourselves as we really are and feel the acceptance of the One who loves us no matter what.[2]

Journal writing can provide the following benefits:

- bring perspective to emotions safely and effectively
- promote meditation and prayer time
- give an overview to the day's activities and evening's thankfulness
- bring a release from stress and anxiety
- unfold new insights and deeper understanding of God's Word

You don't need to aspire to be a writer—just be a pursuer of wisdom. Keep a notebook with you at all times—you never know when you will have the opportunity to commune with and acknowledge God in this way. One day my car got a flat tire on the freeway. After I walked to the nearest gas station to call my beloved husband for help, I had the chance to journal the experience while I waited for my knight to arrive on his white steed.

A—Ask. Microsoft had an advertising campaign that asked, "Where do you want to go today?" Technology has the ability to so expand our world that in a few keystrokes on the computer, we can access almost anything in the world. But accessing God is the key to bountiful living. One morning as I was gazing at the picture of Christ I often use for meditation, I found myself looking into His eyes and saying, "Where do You want me to go today?" We acknowledge God when we put ourselves wholly at His disposal and walk where He needs us to walk, say what He needs us to say, do what He needs us to do. The result is often contented hearts at the end of the day as we lay our heads to rest saying, "Boy, today turned out to be a lot different than I thought it might, but I sure feel good about what happened."

Y—Yak. God enjoys a good chat just as much as the next... uh...person. He says, "Call to me and I will answer you" (Jeremiah 33:3) and "Come now, let us reason together"

(Isaiah 1:18). My good friend Karen calls me several times a week just because she always seems to have something to share. Her daughter is an excellent gymnast, her home-based business is going very well, and she often has amusing insights to pass along. When she calls, we just chat. We catch each other up on the little happening of the days, be they happy or challenging. Over the years, these little chats have helped us form quite a friendship. Without them, we would lose touch and not know the quirky little nuances that keep us honest about ourselves and our day-to-day interactions.

In the moments when you simply acknowledge that God is with you—when you realize that He already knows what you're thinking (so you may as well openly share and discuss it), your relationship with Him deepens, and it becomes increasingly easy to walk hand-in-hand with Him. Chat with Him on a regular and natural basis.

This all adds up to **PRAY.** Prayer is how we live our lives with God. Do we split God off from our senses, our talents, our goals and dreams, and our routine communication? Or can we, with gratitude and relief, rest with the psalmist who says,

> O LORD, you have searched me and you know me. You know when I sit and when I rise; you perceive my thoughts from afar. You discern my going out and my lying down; you are familiar with all my ways. Before a word is on my tongue you know it completely, O LORD. You hem me in—behind and before; you have laid your hand upon me. Such knowledge is too wonderful for me, too lofty for me to attain (139:1-6).

Pray with your life, not just your head. Make it a practice in the morning and in the evening to "bookend" your day with prayer. In the morning look for guidance; in the evening express your gratitude. Orient yourself to be in constant communication

already there—God's presence, comfort, guidance, and companionship. When we do the work of making the investment, we are eliminating all the things that keep us from understanding and receiving God.

The benefit is that we can lay anything before the Lord and count on Him to guide our paths. Are finances a puzzle? Are you at the end of your rope with your children, your neighbor, or your spouse? What is the next career or ministry step for you? Should you say yes to being on that committee or becoming chairman of that board? How should you best share the joy you are feeling over a significant rite of passage? Do you stay in this house or find something else? What do you do with this catastrophic loss? What is the next step in this significant relationship?

The directions God gives are clear. They surface and resurface above all of the "chatter" in our heads. Some directions will be compelling and will need to be acted on obediently in short order, such as Jonah's call to Ninevah (Jonah 1–2). Other directions will unfold over time, as was the path of Joseph from despised brother to dear benefactor (Genesis 37, 39–45). Remember, as God is unfolding things for us, He's directing and leading the paths of thousands of others. The orchestration may take some earthly time to come to fruition!

Some directions will make your heart sing! You will be so relieved and astounded to see the hand of God sweeping through your situation. When I received the confirmation that it was time to start writing and speaking, I felt incredible liberation and glee. Since the time of that call, a number of people have commented on the change in my demeanor. Peacefulness has come over me, filling my soul.

Some directions will break your heart for that season in time. Those times in particular you will want to heavily rely on the promise that as you are obedient, God is competent and reliable to lovingly and wisely direct your life. You may have experienced what I lived through in college. Because I attended a Christian college and was just shy of 20 years old, I assumed that everything that happened in the sacred bubble of my campus was thoroughly ordained by God to be exactly the way it appeared. And I assumed it was all permanent, no questions asked. That included falling head-over-heels in love with an absolutely wonderful man!

As the relationship unfolded, however, it became painfully apparent that our future lives were going to take us in very separate directions. But how could this be? I would sit in our chapel on campus in absolute agony and pray, "God, why did you so powerfully bring us together, why did you let me fall so hopelessly in love with him if he's not the one I'm supposed to marry?" God still gave me the choice, and God rules and overrules, so He would have made the best out of what I chose. However, I still knew in my heart of hearts that it was not going to be in the best interest of either my friend or me to enter into the sacred and beautiful covenant of marriage. The path certainly seemed cruel to me. But I had to give God time for the fuller path to be revealed.

Your path in question may include a career change, a child who falls terminally ill, a friend who turns out to be something other than what you anticipated. God only expects that we trust, give way to His insight, and call on Him for the next minute.

You may find you have an experience like Jill had that really tested her reliance on the promise of Proverbs 3:5-6:

> One life-changing event that required these promises of God to take over in my life was when my husband, Tim, and I experienced the painful road of infertility. For as long as I could remember, I wanted to be a mom. That was my life goal, my career path, the desire of my heart. As I allowed God's plan, His abundant plan, to unfold, we met our future daughter's birth mother and began walking the straight path that God promised us all along in His Word. I am so very blessed to be

Hanna's mom. The relationship God has given me with the amazing woman who gave birth to her is priceless. Trusting God with this desire of my heart and seeing Him come through in the way He did makes me eagerly anticipate what paths He will take me down in the future.

We often find ourselves waiting in the area of career direction. Gaye Lindfors, owner of Significant Solutions, describes her experience:

> Like many of my colleagues and friends, success was defined by my title, perks, salary, and place on the organizational chart. By those definitions, I was doing quite well. I was director of Human Resources for an international Fortune 500 company, servicing a business unit of 11,000 employees. But my heart longed to do something else; something I could not yet define. I just knew I had to do "it."
>
> For two years I prayed that God would allow me to leave my corporate job behind and live my calling—my purpose for being placed on this earth. I knew that my mission was to highlight, celebrate, and inspire significance in myself and others, but I didn't know how to live that out on a daily basis. I also knew that I could not do this in my current employment situation. But for two years His answer was clearly no. Until one Friday morning in early September 2002. During a team leadership meeting filled with frustration, anger, and finger-pointing, I sat quietly and realized, "It's time to go." I was immediately filled with peace. God's time had come. And seven weeks later, I was a very happy, reenergized, unemployed middle-aged woman who set off to live the life she was meant to live.
>
> I feel I demonstrated wisdom in three specific ways:

1. I waited on God. I could have easily justified leaving my employer much earlier, but I waited for God's perfect timing.

2. I did not panic. No job—no income—no problem. I clung to Proverbs 3:5-6. I knew His plan for my life would be revealed.

3. I asked a very wise woman to walk with me on this part of my journey. Robin used and shared her wisdom to guide me through a very exciting, yet challenging transition.

Sometimes our wisdom is best demonstrated by waiting. And sometimes it is best demonstrated by sharing it with others.

The Ultimate Source of Wisdom

Looking through Scripture, we find that the Holy Spirit is often coupled with the attribute of wisdom. We see that wisdom, like all spiritual gifts, is given through the Spirit (1 Corinthians 12:8). Men who were identified as wise were described as being full of the Spirit and wisdom (Acts 6:3). Paul asks that his friends be given the Spirit of wisdom and revelation so that they may know God better (Ephesians 1:17). The beautiful description of the Suffering Servant in Isaiah says, "The Spirit of the LORD will rest on him—the Spirit of wisdom and of understanding, the Spirit of counsel and of power, the Spirit of knowledge and of the fear of the LORD" (11:2).

Being attuned to God's Holy Spirit is the key to gaining wisdom. As Paul seems to indicate to the church at Corinth, obtaining wisdom comes as we grow in our faith, becoming more solid because of our deeper understanding of God and His ways:

We, of course, have plenty of wisdom to pass on to you once you get your feet on firm spiritual ground, but it's not popular wisdom, the fashionable wisdom of high-priced experts that will be out-of-date in a year or so. God's wisdom is something mysterious that goes deep into the interior of his purposes. You don't find it lying around on the surface. It's not the latest message, but more like the oldest—what God determined as the way to bring out his best in us, long before we ever arrived on the scene. The experts of our day haven't a clue about what this eternal plan is. If they had, they wouldn't have killed the Master of the God-designed life on a cross. That's why we have this Scripture text:

No one's ever seen or heard anything like this,
    Never so much as imagined anything quite like it—
    What God has arranged for those who love him.
    But you've seen and heard it because God by his Spirit has brought it all out into the open before you.
    The Spirit, not content to flit around on the surface, dives into the depths of God, and brings out what God planned all along (1 Corinthians 2:6-10 MSG).

My favorite way to think about the closeness and immediacy of the Holy Spirit is to imagine radio waves and what it takes to tune in to them. Radio waves are around us all the time. The air is teeming with radio waves being sent out by thousands of stations, just looking for someone who has the dial tuned to their frequencies. Similarly, I think of the need to tune my radio to God's frequency in the form of the Holy Spirit. I am always comforted to think of the Spirit as being as close as my breathing and as constant as my heartbeat.

God's Holy Spirit is so close and so desirous of helping that we can sometimes be surprised by how quickly guidance and direction come. Debbie tells of a time when she had such an experience:

> I do not believe that many of my shining moments as a woman of wisdom have been completely driven by my own wisdom. I believe that many of these situations were driven by God speaking through me. For example, a friend of mind was trying to get pregnant. They were married in June and had been trying since their wedding night. Around Christmas she sent me an email telling me that she felt guilty for being a bit jealous of a friend who got pregnant on the first try. She couldn't understand why God would put such a strong longing in her heart to have children if she was unable. She had so many emotions rushing through her and felt guilty for it. I told her that God wouldn't have given us emotions if he didn't intend for us to experience them. She told me that made her feel so much better. After the conversation ended, I sat there in awe as to where my response came from. That is when I realized that God was using me to help ease my friend's anxiety and guilt.

This sense of Spirit-driven intuition is underscored by a beautiful psalm, "Surely you desire truth in the inner parts; you teach me wisdom in the inmost place" (51:6).

My own understanding of this process came one evening while tucking my daughter into bed. Ever since she was a baby, Madison has been one of those kids who is wide awake at night. As an extrovert, she doesn't want to go to sleep for fear she'll miss something going on in the world. As a bright child, her mind is always thinking, planning, and designing. But in all this she felt a little bit like a freak.

I sat with her, talking about this for the umpteenth time. I was tired, she was tired, and we were both tired of her feeling like this was a problem. We had talked about it many times before and in so many ways with me offering suggestions.

I sent up one of those silent prayers mommies often pray, "Help. Just a few good words of wisdom would be appreciated."

I had been talking to one of my communication classes earlier that day about personal preferences. That's when the still, small voice suggested I frame this situation in terms of personal preference. I offered to Madison that her nighttime ritual was not some weird and strange personality flaw, but simply a preference. Some people can fall asleep as soon as their heads hit the pillow; some take a little longer to go to sleep because they like to think about things a few extra minutes.

She quieted and then said, "Do you really think that's what's happening with me?"

I said to her, "Yes." I said to the Holy Spirit, "Thank You."

Which Way Do You Lean?

In which direction does your heart tilt? Are you a "Jezebel," with plans, designs, and dreams that don't include God? Or have you turned your heart, your soul, your mind, and your strength over to the gracious, perfect, and exciting direction of God? Chances are very good that you are somewhere in the middle. My prayer for you is that as you read, reflect on, and apply the wisdom in this book, you will be moved to decide more and more for God each day.

GOING DEEPER

Warm-up: Consider this quote by William Law: "Devotion is neither private nor public prayer, but a life given to God." What do you think he means?

1. How would you describe Jezebel in contemporary language?

2. How would you describe the Original Wise Woman in modern terms?

3. The bottom line in Proverbs 3:5-6 is the simple description of walking hand in hand with God. Simple isn't always easy, though. What do you see as the difference between simple and easy?

4. In the definition of trust as competence and reliability, what does competence mean to you? When has God shown Himself to be competent in your life? Do you have a favorite biblical passage or verse that underscores God's competence?

5. Describe a time when you benefited or were blessed by God's reliability. What are some other words that come to mind that are the same as "reliable"? Identify a biblical character or passage you relate to when identifying the reliability of God in your own life.

6. Is it hard for you to trust? Why or why not? Although you may not share it aloud in a group, it is critical for your growth as a woman of wisdom to identify any "trust blocks" and to take steps to eliminate them. Ask God's Spirit to assist you in this, and seek the counsel of trusted advisors and/or professionals as needed.

7. In all your ways acknowledge God. How does your life reflect your relationship with God in manner, means, miles, and milieu?

8. Look back through these ways and do an inventory. How would you acknowledge God in each of them? What do you want to keep? What do you want to change? What would you add that is not mentioned in the book?

9. How do we acknowledge God?

   a.

   b.

   c.

   d.

   Based on this list, which one would you like to concentrate on for the week? How will you implement this? Can you think of other ways you or others "acknowledge" God?

10. If the Holy Spirit is like radio waves moving through the air waiting for those who are picking up the right frequencies, how can you clean off your God receptors to receive a stronger signal?

Assignment for this week: Construct a poem about God's presence in your life. Use traditional rhyme, haiku, a picture poem, an acrostic, or free verse.

3

YOUR INDUSTRIAL REVOLUTION

Teach us to number our days aright, that we may gain a heart of wisdom.

Spiritual life is a matter of becoming who you truly are. It's not becoming Catherine of Siena, or some other saint, but who you are. It sounds easy enough, but being who you truly are is work, courage and faith.

RICHARD ROHR

It happens at least once a month. I receive in the mail a flyer promising me that if I attend a certain seminar or all-day workshop, I will become a better manager of time, projects, and people. The brochure assures me that I will become masterful at getting more accomplished in a day—I will have the ability to tackle multiple tasks and be more productive in the number of items I can check off my to-do list.

It wasn't until I had taken a course or two like this that I realized the ironic truth: I don't want to do more in my day! I want to do less! What I want more of is some sense of meaning and cohesion in what I do. I want to live my life on purpose, not just running about checking things off a list, lengthening my resumé, or playing supermom!

Do less? I thought. *Am I nuts? I'll never get anywhere in this life if I do less! My children will be undereducated, under-stimulated, and generally unfit to enter the college of our choice. My house will be a wreck, and my nails will be a sight. I won't have people recognize me at the store for all the benevolent work I've done in the community or the advances I've made in my career! What was I thinking?*

But I was suffering from being a choice-aholic. There were too many choices in my life, and they were all so tempting. With each new choice I felt more drawn to something better, something bigger, something that would make my life richer or easier. Soon I was chasing every option that came my way with no sense of who I truly was in the first place. I was the one to whom James referred—tossed about by every wave of alternative only to find myself breathless and disoriented as I was smashed on the shore (James 1:6).

The personal Industrial Revolution is about doing less in life, not more. If you are weary of management specialists who say they can help you although they have never met you, they don't know your situation, and they don't understand your personality, take heart. The greatest management specialist of them all knows your design and your path intimately. If you are tired of "too much," the way of wisdom will clarify, simplify, and affirm your deep longing to live at peace with who the Almighty fashioned you to be. As we look at what it means to be a wise woman in a wild world by letting God work through you, we will explore doing less in a day, but doing it with more passion, purpose, and power than ever before. Your days will become more satisfying; your life will become more congruent.

Internal or External Motivation?

Many of us feel unproductive or unfulfilled even when we are running from the time our feet hit the floor in the morning to the time we collapse into bed at night. Women, especially, are flying through the day at a breakneck pace to carry out volunteer commitments, get the kids where they need to be, manage and meet work deadlines and obligations, keep everyone and everything in the house reasonably clean and neat, and maybe squeeze in some exercise or prayer on a sporadic basis. I know very few lazy women.

I do know a fair number of women who are really busy but burned out, despondent, unfocused, missionless—and some who are downright depressed as they look at the unfolding day and wonder, "Am I just going to do yesterday all over again?" These women lack direction, design, and determination because they don't have the control and order that wisdom brings to life. Busyness can be a symptom of a deeper uneasiness. Busyness often has two root causes: general anxiety and fear of what others are going to say about us.

We live in troubled times, and it's hard to be still when we are highly anxious. On a large scale, our general anxiety may stem from all the bad news reported by the media. On a more personal level, anxiety may come from a sense of being out of control of our finances, calendar, and future. General anxiety may also be rooted in a vague sense that we just aren't enough. To fill the uneasy gaps, we stay busy.

Another specific and prevalent worry is the fear of what others are going to say about us. How do our careers stack up against other people's? How do people view our decisions or choices regarding our children, spouses, houses, volunteer commitments, clothing, financial situations, faith walks, social circles...and on and on and on. We can run ourselves ragged in the relentless pursuit of having as much as, if not more than, the Joneses. We see it all the time. One neighbor signs little Agnes up for cheerleading camp, and next thing you know, all the little girls in the neighborhood are signed up for cheerleading camp. Sheila at work has moved into a very comfortable new condo complex. Suddenly everyone is checking into the rates at that complex. Sarah, in the Monday-morning

Bible study, has signed up to help in the hospital guild, and a week later the whole group has volunteered to help in the hospital—especially if it's "the place to be" for seeing and being seen. We stay busy to keep the little devils of comparison at arm's length.

The lengths to which we will go to "stay busy" and keep up the pretense that life is fulfilling are remarkable. In 1980, the movie *Ordinary People* starred Academy Award-nominated Mary Tyler Moore as a mother who had lost her beloved older son to a boating accident. The strain of the loss wore on her, her husband, and their surviving son, who believed he had caused the death. Her son went through extensive therapy. Her husband handled his grief as authentically as he could. She stayed busy, unable to forgive her younger son and move successfully through her grief. To keep her overwhelming anxiety at bay, she insulated herself with possessions and suburban activities. In the end, as father and son became more real, she chose to leave the family, not wanting to let down the façade of pristine perfection and the veneer of invulnerability.

We sometimes trade activity for truth, appearances for integrity, accolades for the souls of our families and our very selves.

Being busy can signal an emphasis on external motivation or feeling compelled to satisfy the demands and expectations of others around us.

The opposite of being externally motivated to be busy is being a woman who actively walks in step with the Master—who knows who she is and whose she is. Instead of racing to and fro in disjointed endeavors, trying to keep up with life, the wise woman lives a life of centered intentionality and peace. She moves through her days with a sense of divine mission. Being active marks the woman who moves from her internal center, the place where she and God have communicated with one another about what she is to be about. This center is the place from which she structures her plans, commitments, activities, and relationships. The active wise woman is internally motivated, compelled by her desire to please God first.

Being active can be hard work as we put aside what others think of us, say no to temptations that will make us "busy," and concentrate on the essence of what God calls us to be. The hard work is to get back to basics, to critically think about all the input we are constantly receiving, and to use a clear head and a clear heart in deciding what we believe and who we are. We have a choice. We can be genuinely and serenely tired from the hard work of being true to God and to ourselves, or we can be perpetually exhausted from endlessly chasing the approval of others.

Actively walking with the Master instead of being burned out with busyness is a continuous process. I definitely have overly busy, externally motivated days when I have to catch my breath, say a prayer, and try to get back on the internally motivated active track. Thank God the Holy Spirit sticks close and lets me know when I'm getting out of sync with the beautiful pace God intends for me.

In a world filled with choices, understanding and living our essence in Christ will keep us from becoming overwhelmed, buried, defeated, and despondent. That is the loving design of a very wise God.

Desert Essence

Perhaps the most striking biblical account of someone living with focus and purpose stemming from a clearly understood essence is Jesus' meeting with Satan in the desert. This encounter is documented in three of the four Gospels, but most extensively in Matthew 4:1-11:

> Then Jesus was led by the Spirit into the desert to
> be tempted by the devil. After fasting forty days
> and forty nights, he was hungry. The tempter came
> to him and said, "If you are the Son of God, tell
> these stones to become bread." Jesus answered, "It

is written: 'Man does not live on bread alone, but on every word that comes from the mouth of God.' "

Then the devil took him to the holy city and had him stand on the highest point of the temple. "If you are the Son of God," he said, "throw yourself down. For it is written: 'He will command his angels concerning you, and they will lift you up in their hands, so that you will not strike your foot against a stone.'" Jesus answered him, "It is also written: 'Do not put the Lord your God to the test.'"

Again, the devil took him to a very high mountain and showed him all the kingdoms of the world and their splendor. "All this I will give you," he said, "if you bow down and worship me." Jesus said to him, "Away from me, Satan! For it is written: 'Worship the Lord your God, and serve him only.'" Then the devil left him, and angels came and attended him.

Provision, protection, possessions. Satan knows how to hit us right where we are vulnerable. He knows there are many slick little ways he can tempt us to give up our God-given identities and purpose. The master deceiver knows how to mask huge sinkholes with lush, green grass and beautiful wildflowers. Let's look at each trap for what it really is.

Provision. The tempter knew precisely where Jesus was vulnerable. Jesus had been fasting 40 days. For many of us, 40 minutes without some kind of snack is a stretch! Jesus was hungry—very hungry. So Satan offered Him the opportunity to eat. Satan extended the invitation to satisfy a need, a worthy need, in exchange for His understanding of His higher call.

We have many needs, including security, food, shelter, clothing, affection, and a sense of being valued and appreciated.

Satisfying needs is not in and of itself evil. The *means* by which we satisfy our needs can be.

Satan tempted Jesus to change the nature of things in order to satisfy His needs. Satan loves nothing more than for what God created to be of one essence—to be beautiful and holy—to transform into something ordinary or base to satiate our needs. The world changes the nature of needs to wants, and then invites us to change the things around us and ourselves to meet those wants. For instance, we are invited to change ourselves from the temple of the Holy Spirit to a sexual object to meet needs for affection, acceptance, and love. We are encouraged to change our children into recreated images of ourselves to satisfy our needs for approval, validation, and immortality. We exchange a carefree childhood and the joy of discovery for an endless string of activities and stimulation to "prepare them for their future." We are enticed to take a higher-paying job that does not match our call, our mission, or our interests to make more money because we "need" a better quality of home, food, clothing, or social outlet.

What God created to be one thing, we change to something else because we cannot or will not wait for or accept His provision.

Jesus knew that He must not change those stones, must not alter their God-given essence. He let Satan know that He would not compromise Himself or God's creation to miss out on the higher banquet awaiting Him in God's kingdom.

Protection. At first blush, this temptation appears to be Satan's urge to Jesus to save Himself from bodily harm. Satan is encouraging Jesus to put aside what He already knows about God's care for Him and to test it one more time. "Let's just see if God will protect You one more time; after all, You are God's Son."

A closer look reveals Satan is calling on Jesus to protect His name, to defend His reputation, to cement His place in the world. Jesus is being solicited to prove what He already knows about Himself and His loving, heavenly Father. Satan wants Jesus to be lured into a competition, a childish game of "prove it."

Anytime you sense a dare, a temptation to do something because it will prove who you are, *run*—do not walk—*away!* Games of "prove it" often start with phrases like, "If you're really a Christian..." "If you were a good employee, wife, mother, member of the community, woman, friend..." Anytime you are asked to trade your understanding of your God-given essence to protect your name, reputation, or public standing, you can be assured you are being enticed to trade your identity for something inferior.

Possessions. This one seems rather obvious. After all, people with their heads on straight and their feet firmly planted in Proverbs 3:5-6 could see this one coming a mile off! Because Satan knows it is "useless to spread a net in full view of the birds" (Proverbs 1:17), he asks us to trade our essence for possessions in very subtle ways.

Satan urged Christ to simply bow down, just this once, to worship him. This small investment would net Him all the kingdoms of the world and their splendor. This ten-second act seems a small price to pay for eternal riches. Satan actually wanted Jesus to worship him, and Jesus wasn't falling for it. Jesus says straight out of God's Word, "Worship the LORD your God, and serve him only" (Deuteronomy 6:13).

Jesus knows what appears to be a slight nod in Satan's direction will turn into a lifetime of slavery. What Satan paints as a small act, bowing down, is unmasked as cancerous servitude.

Have you traded your sense of integrity for a moment of entitlement? Have you given a small wink to Satan by choosing just for a moment to worship an earthly passion, only to have shackles clamped on your soul? Have you said yes to possessions or actions that are now ruling your life, eating up your time, and destroying your peace of mind? What we sometimes overlook is the enormous upkeep involved with owning the kingdoms of this world and their splendor. It takes a great deal of time and money to polish, repair, dust, clean, mow, maintain, and weed these kingdoms. One day we wake up and realize we have, along with all our stuff, an empty feeling, a sense that something is missing. Our mission and satisfaction have disappeared.

Act, Love, Walk

The secret to walking with the Master in step with Wisdom and having the ability to say no to temptation and yes to our essence is to get back to basics and understand the foundational characteristics God has formed in us. We need to comprehend and live the unavoidable call of God on our lives.

By "call" I don't mean career path or what we get accomplished. By "call" I don't even mean our spiritual gifts and what we feel we need to do to serve God. By "call," I mean how we are to live our lives as we go about doing all of the things that we do. When we pay close attention to how we do what we do, we find that we are doing with more intentionality, with more dignity, and with greater alignment to God's purposes. As we live life with this kind of godly intentionality, we find that the "what" we are supposed to do unfolds more naturally and with less angst and stress as we focus on the "how" we are supposed to do.

When I ask people about God's call on their lives, more often than not, they think of "call" as a job, a career, or something they "do" with their lives. As a life-direction consultant, I work with many people each year helping them discern their particular and personal paths in life. What does God want them to do? What job should they take? What's the purpose of their lives, and how can they most distinctly and authentically pursue it? We all want to be distinct and make our individual mark on the world. Yet it's so easy to get caught up in being a unique expression of who we are and what we should be doing that we forget there are some beautiful basics that God has called each of us to pursue. The essence of what God calls us to is indispensable and necessary if we want to feel fully alive and completely whole.

Recently my family was sitting at the dinner table and my daughter wanted to hear the family go around the table and tell her what we thought she ought to do with her life. Her father, her brother, and I all gave our opinions based on talents, interests, and passions we have seen her exhibit. We were talking about her career and her future. And she was feeling frustrated because she has so many talents and interests that she was getting overloaded. She moaned at one point, "What am I supposed to do?"

Then it hit me. The call of God is not on what my children are supposed to do with their lives in the future. The call of God is on what He wants them to *be* today and tomorrow, not on what he wants them to *do*. I offered this perspective to her, "Honey, the turns in the road ahead will make themselves apparent, but God is calling you to some rather remarkable things right this very minute, like loving your family, being nice to your little brother, and enjoying and using the talents He has given you right now. Your call in life is expressed right now and tomorrow when you go to school. Live that well, and you will never be without purpose."

I remember feeling the same way in college. Although I had declared my major and was enjoying my course of study, I was still unclear about my career. Being a working woman and having a career that made me important in my own right was very high on my list of priorities at that point, but I still didn't feel like I knew exactly what I should be doing after college. I kept asking, "What does God want me to do?" I was distressed.

Then I ran into a friend who really annoyed me with his counsel. As we were talking about my distress, he challenged me with this thought: How was I doing with the basics of my spiritual life? This annoyed me for two reasons. I felt like I had that handled pretty well, and I didn't know what in the world this had to do with my career. I was pretty clueless about authentic spiritual living back then.

So my friend offered me a beautiful little thought from Micah: "He has showed you, O man, what is good. And what does the LORD require of you? To act justly and to love mercy and to walk humbly with your God" (6:8). The question I had to wrestle with at that point was this: Am I so focused on what God wants me to *do* in the future that I have blown by what God wants me to *be* today?

James offers us a beautiful portrait of the essence of wisdom: "But the wisdom that comes from heaven is first of all pure; then peace-loving, considerate, submissive, full of mercy and good fruit, impartial and sincere. Peacemakers who sow in peace raise a harvest of righteousness" (James 3:17-18).

Wisdom Basics

James 3:17-18 gives us a lovely checklist of wisdom traits that we can pursue any time in life, in any place of work, in any relationships we have. A wise woman in a wild world is...

Pure. This word has three connotations. The first is unmixed or uncluttered. A wise woman who is pure is free from distractions and unhealthy alliances. Second, purity is about an all-out character that is utterly who she is. She isn't halfway. She is full out and downright in her convictions and personality. She is totally authentic. Third, a woman of wisdom who is pure seeks to keep the channels open between herself and her God, preferring to live a life as free from sin as possible, marked by being at one with God.

Peace-loving. A wise woman is harmonious in her relationships. Harmony allows for all the notes in the symphony to be played—they just need to be played in a way that is not offensive to the ear. Harmony brings out the best in each note, making them together something that each of them couldn't be alone. To live in harmony and peace doesn't mean to live in absolute agreement. It means to seek the best in everyone and everything, and help them all work together for an overall good. This peace-loving woman of wisdom knows that you can disagree without being disagreeable.

Considerate. Gentleness marks the life of a wise woman. She is respectful, gracious, tactful, and thoughtful. She may be a very boisterous, larger-than-life woman, yet she has a grace about her that puts people at ease. Being considerate is more about tone than volume.

Submissive. One who is submissive is open to reason and willing to yield. The term "submissive" has been used on women for generations to mean giving in to the wishes of others, especially male authority figures. But the passage in James obviously calls for a submissive spirit in *both* genders. The person with a submissive spirit is reasonable, willing to listen, and not demanding his or her own way or the exclusivity of his or her own voice. It's an approach to conversation and relationship rather than an end result of gender, race, or age factors in a relationship.

Merciful. Are you forgiving, compassionate, kind, and charitable? If you are, you're a woman answering the most basic of calls God gives to us. Jesus was called "Christ the power of God and the wisdom of God" (1 Corinthians 1:24). The very essence of Jesus' life was forgiveness, compassion, and kindness. As an embodiment of the very wisdom of God, Jesus gave us a remarkable model of what it means to be wise.

Impartial. The wise woman is equitable and fair. She seeks to be objective in conflict, giving everyone a chance to speak. She doesn't prefer one class over another, one gender over another, one race over another, or one age over another. She is wise in the way she acts toward an outsider, whomever the outsider may be considered to be at any given point (Colossians 4:5). She treats everyone with respect, knowing that all are created by God.

Sincere. Without hypocrisy, a wise woman is real, straightforward, candid, and forthright. She is trustworthy because what you see is what you get, what you hear is what she thinks, and what she promises is going to come to fruition.

"ESSENCE" TREASURE HUNT

The beginning of understanding what you are to do in life is to understand what you are to be. How aligned are you with the basics of what it means to be a wise woman in a wild world? Use the following scale in responding to each statement:

5=always   4=often   3=sometimes   2=rarely   1=never

_____ 1. I live a pure life in the sense that it is free from fleshly obsessions and unhealthy alliances.

_____ 2. I live a pure life in the sense that I am authentic and genuine. What you see is what I am.

_____ 3. I live a pure life in the sense that I keep the channels open with God by seeking to understand and eliminate sin in my life.

_____ 4. I seek harmony, realizing that people can disagree without being disagreeable.

_____ 5. I am considerate, tactful, and gracious.

_____ 6. I am willing to listen, not demanding that my own voice be the only one that is heard.

_____ 7. I am merciful by being forgiving, compassionate, and charitable.

_____ 8. I treat everyone the same, knowing that all are created by God.

_____ 9. I am candid, straightforward, and forthright.

The higher your score on this scale of 9 to 45, the more you are preparing the way to find out what you are to *do* in life by embracing and practicing what you are to *be*.

Becoming Wise

Incorporating the "Wisdom Basics" into your life builds positive character and provides direction. You are more likely to clearly understand the will of God for specifics such as career and relationship choices when you understand first the will of God for your character. What wisdom traits need to be a larger part of your life? In what particular situations do you find it hard to live the essence of wisdom? How can you address those situations?

Pure. Peace-loving. Considerate. Submissive. Merciful. Impartial. Sincere.

When we look at a list of characteristics like this, it is tempting to respond in several negative ways. The first is to become discouraged by thinking we will never fully succeed in living out these traits. And we won't if we're depending on ourselves to make the changes. We most certainly must be open to the changes occurring, but it happens only through an intimate partnership with the Holy Spirit. It's like the commercials where a dangerous act is taking place, or television shows where kids are involved in extreme sports. The disclaimer is always "Don't try this on your own!" Pursuing a life of wisdom is an extreme sport. Don't attempt it without God.

Pursuing a life of wisdom is an extreme sport. Don't attempt it without God.

The second is to think these characteristics are going to look exactly the same in everyone. Each person "should" be displaying them in just the "right" and prescribed way. While the call on each of our lives is to live these basics, the way they are expressed in each of us will be as distinct as we are. While we were all made in the image of God, we were each made to represent God a little differently than anyone else. What living these attributes means for a quiet and reserved person may look completely different if the same trait is being expressed in an extrovert. Someone who leads with her head is going to express sincerity differently than someone who leads with her heart. A wise woman understands we are all different. She expresses these traits to her fullest ability without worrying about how anyone else is doing!

The third negative response is to get a little smug if we start to excel in one or more of the traits and look down on others who aren't quite where we are yet. It doesn't take much insight to realize, however, that the moment we step into that realm, we have stepped out of wisdom's light expressed by the very traits we're pursuing.

Our wild world places a heap of importance on attainment, achievement, success, and accomplishment. We are tempted to be always looking at the noteworthy, the sensational, or the newsmakers. If we are looking to career, success, our family, or our possessions as a barometer of how we're living the life God wants us to live, we will find big holes in our satisfaction levels and big gaps in the timeline of feeling like we're doing something worthwhile.

Consider a car that is out of alignment. Even though it is carrying out its purpose, it isn't doing so with smoothness and efficiency. You may be in the misaligned car traveling the road to a destination, but if it is shaking and rattling it's not going to be a comfortable ride for you, and it certainly isn't good for the car, either. Your Industrial Revolution—being able to move through your life with effectiveness and joy—is dependent on how well you master and embody the basics that God intends for everyone, as well as seeking the unique expression of your life purpose and your gifts. When we get back to the basics and look at what God wants us to do with our character instead of our career, we find we are never "out of work" and always up to something worthwhile.

Wise women know that while a career or work path has turns in the road throughout life, the call to lovely character always remains. Wise women know they can always trust that as long as they lean on God's gracious providence in the big picture and acknowledge Him in every moment of every day, their paths and steps will be just where they ought to be.

That is peace, passion, and purpose. Put that in a brochure and mail it!

GOING DEEPER

Warm-up: Give thought to the distinction between being busy and being active. What does your life feel and look like when you are busy? What does your life feel and look like when you are active?

1. What do you need to do to start your own Industrial Revolution?

2. Most of us vacillate between being externally "busy" and being internally in tune with God. Where are you today? Does something need to change?

3. Do you feel alive or like you are just going through the motions? What can you do to become more awake?

4. How does or would implementing the basics of your God-given essence make a difference in the way you live your life?

5. Review the account of Jesus' temptation and the three traps Satan set for Jesus to test His sense of identity or call. If Satan were going to come to you and offer you a trade for your God-given essence, what would he most likely offer that would tempt you most? If you are in a group and feel comfortable, share an experience you have had with this and what you learned from it.

Assignment for this week: There are seven qualities listed under the subhead "Wisdom Basics." Choose one each day on which to focus. Write it on a card and tape it to your dashboard, mirror, computer monitor, or kitchen sink, wherever you are likely to be reminded of it. Keep changing the quality you focus on every day for several weeks. Think about the quality and how you can incorporate it into your daily life.

4

HOW TO HAVE
A SMART MOUTH

*Let your conversation be always full of grace, seasoned with
salt, so that you may know how to answer everyone.*

COLOSSIANS 4:6

*Better to remain silent and be thought a fool, than to speak
out and remove all doubt.*

ABRAHAM LINCOLN

Few things are more sickening than being caught in a lie.
Unless, perhaps, it's having a precious secret blasted throughout
a group. Or maybe it's worse to realize that you have crushed
someone's spirit by speaking harshly in a moment of anger or
frustration? A possible contender would be bragging about
something you've done or obtained, only to see the blank look
of disinterest on other people's faces.

Each of us has a great deal of power. We don't always feel
very powerful, but the fact that we have the resource of language in our lives and people with whom we relate and have
influence means we have power by what we say and what we
don't say.

Our communities are like pieces of fabric. Whenever we use our words for good, we add beauty to the fabric, as with lovely embroidery or exquisite beadwork. When we use our words to harm, we put little holes in the fabric that, over time, become bigger holes that display frayed edges, torn stitches, and sometimes irreparable damage.

There are more references to our communication habits in the wisdom literature, especially Proverbs, than to any other topic mentioned. When seven sins are listed that the Lord finds detestable, three of them have to do directly with the little muscle in our mouths: a lying tongue, a false witness who pours out lies, and a man who stirs up dissension among brothers (Proverbs 6:16-19). Throughout the Gopels and the epistles, many references to how we speak and what we say underscore the potency of the power we have in using our speech wisely. A wise woman in a wild world knows and understands the proper harnessing and use of this power. James 3 illustrates the influence of our speech:

> When we put bits into the mouths of horses to make them obey us, we can turn the whole animal. Or take ships as an example. Although they are so large and are driven by strong winds, they are steered by a very small rudder wherever the pilot wants to go. Likewise the tongue is a small part of the body, but it makes great boasts. Consider what a great forest is set on fire by a small spark. The tongue also is a fire, a world of evil among the parts of the body. It corrupts the whole person, sets the whole course of his life on fire, and is itself set on fire by hell....With the tongue we praise our Lord and Father, and with it we curse men, who have been made in God's likeness. Out of the same mouth come praise and cursing. My brothers, this should not be (verses 3-6,9-10).

Having a smart mouth means you know that every time you open your mouth, you do so for the honor or dishonor of God, and you show yourself to be either a fool or a woman of wisdom. That's a pretty compelling load to bear, when you come right down to it. Little wonder Proverbs 10:19-20 counsels: "The more talk, the less truth; the wise measure their words. The speech of a good person is worth waiting for; the blabber of the wicked is worthless" (MSG). It would be interesting to see what would happen to our wisdom quotient if we simply talked less and prayerfully considered all that comes out of our mouths!

"OUR WORDS" TREASURE HUNT

Answer the following questions quickly, without too much deliberation. How smart is your mouth in these 12 statements? Use the following scale in responding to each statement:

5=always   4=often   3=sometimes   2=rarely   1=never

_____ 1. I think before I speak.

_____ 2. I am an advocate for those who can't speak for themselves.

_____ 3. I keep my promises.

_____ 4. I speak gently.

_____ 5. I give wise instructions.

_____ 6. I speak honestly in love.

_____ 7. I am encouraging.

_____ 8. I don't brag.

_____ 9. I don't gossip.

_____ 10. I am not crass or vulgar.

_____ 11. I self-disclose appropriately.

_____ 12. I know when to keep my mouth shut.

You can have a score between 12 and 60. The higher your score, the likelier you are to have a smart mouth.

Read on in this chapter to find out what it means to have a smart mouth. As you are "Going Deeper" at the end of the chapter, you will have the opportunity to pinpoint the ways you are a woman of wise speech as well as identify more completely the areas that need work.

The Dynamic Dozen of Wise Speech

Consider these top 12 ways to get a smart mouth. As you read through this chapter, remember that your intrapersonal communication, or how you speak and listen to yourself, is as powerful (if not more so) as your interpersonal communication, or how you speak and listen to others. Practice having a smart mouth in both realms.

1. *Think before you speak.*

It happens every day in homes with small children. A youngster begins a sentence with, "I have a great idea!" Because of a schedule crunch or a tense mood in the home, a parent or grandparent will say, "No!" If that happens in my house, my daughter stamps her foot and says, "Mommy, you didn't even listen to what I was going to say." And most of the time she's right. And when I got my head into the current moment and listened to what she had to say, sometimes it really was a great idea! It led to something fun, the expedition of a task, or to a special moment together. Every time I do this, I think of the proverb, "If one gives answer before he hears, it is his folly and shame" (Proverbs 18:13 RSV).

Even more humiliating and foolish is barking a reply in a heated moment that causes the emotional temperature to rise further. "A fool gives full vent to his anger, but a wise man keeps himself under control" (Proverbs 29:11). As an experiment for one month, try taking a deep breath, lowering your voice, and softening your eyes every time you feel the kettle brewing. See if it doesn't facilitate a better understanding between all involved.

Proverbs 15:28 says, "The heart of the righteous weighs its answers, but the mouth of the wicked gushes evil." Be a woman who thinks before she speaks, who forms a complete and loving answer. The best way to think before you speak is to be sure the other person has finished completely what he or she is saying!

2. Be an advocate.

Wise speech meets loving service with world-changing results when you become an advocate for those who cannot speak for themselves. In Proverbs 31:8, King Lemuel's mother admonishes him: "Speak up for those who cannot speak for themselves, for the rights of all who are destitute. Speak up and judge fairly; defend the rights of the poor and needy."

Your speech is supremely wise when you use God's gift of your tongue to do the work of the Lord for peace and justice. Many people in our world, because of handicap, age, or social disparity cannot speak for themselves. Or if they can and do, they are dismissed because they are perceived to be inferior or ineffective by those who have the power to change the situation of those who plead.

Who in your world cannot speak for themselves? Who is in need of mercy, justice, assistance, or love? Could you be called to be a champion for the children of your church before a governing body? Maybe you are to promote the rights of someone you love as she lies dying or is in need of medical treatment. Does your elderly neighbor need an ally? Do the refugees on the television need an advocate? What's happening in the downtown area of your city or town? Is there a need for you to speak up for the rights of the poor, the undereducated, or the imprisoned right in your own backyard?

A friend told me of an experience she had in a local large grocery store. She was standing in a regular nonexpress checkout line that was positioned next to a 15-item-limit express line. She witnessed the clerk asking a gentleman who was in the express line if he had more than 15 items. His response was, "Who are you, the warden?" She pointed out to him that the line he was in was an express lane, and because there were other customers behind him in line, his violation was holding them up. His reply was, "I have been coming to this store for years. Of course I know this is an express line." He then tossed his check-cashing card at her and revealed to her that he was a personal friend of the prominent owner of this particular grocery chain.

All in all, my friend was disgusted by the customer's rude and arrogant behavior, and she felt sorry for the clerk. Once the man had left, my friend tapped the clerk on the shoulder to assure her that at least someone else knew what had happened—that this man had been inappropriate and the clerk had handled the situation as well as she could. The grateful clerk asked if my friend would relay the story to the manager because she was fearful that the man would call the store and try to get her fired.

My friend used the power of speech to be an advocate for the clerk—someone she didn't even know—who needed a voice to speak up on her behalf. Advocacy can be that simple. Search your heart and see if part of your ministry includes advocacy.

3. Keep your promises.

We don't like to think breaking our promises is actually lying. It was an oversight, it slipped our minds, or we just couldn't get to it. But Proverbs 12:22 has this word for would-be promise-keepers: "Lying lips are an abomination to the LORD, but those who act faithfully are his delight" (RSV). Faithfulness in our speech is evidenced when we say what we mean and we mean what we say.

My friend Karen told me of the difference a promise kept can make in a little person's life. She and her son went grocery shopping one evening. Part of that night's bounty was goodies for a packed lunch for school the next day. Michael was excited, looking forward to a special, homemade treat.

The next morning, Karen's household, which includes a very busy husband and three kids, was bedlam. Homework was flying into backpacks, hair was hastily brushed, cereal and milk were flowing at a rapid pace. There was simply no time to pack the much-anticipated expression of a mother's love—the special lunch.

Michael went to the bus a very sad little boy. Big tears flowed as he explained how much he had looked forward to this lunch full of the good things that had so carefully been chosen the night before. Karen has a real soft spot for her children, but she also had physical therapy and a lunch appointment that morning. But the more she thought about it, the more she was convinced that she needed to keep her promise to her son. She packed his little lunch box and drove nearly thirty minutes to deliver the precious, promised lunch. She related later at lunch (which, by the way, she was late for because of the promised delivery!) that she will never forget the look on his face as she walked into the room and handed him his lunch. Not only did Michael become convinced once more of his mother's love for him, he subconsciously reaffirmed that God is faithful and can be trusted.

4. Speak gently.

Proverbs 15:1 says, "A gentle answer turns away wrath, but harsh words cause quarrels" (TLB). You have seen it in your own life. When you are provoked, but you count to ten and speak gently to your provoker, the confrontation is more likely to be resolved than if you answer quickly in a harsh tone.

Speaking more gently as a regular habit will dramatically alter our everyday interactions as those around us realize we are not to be feared or dismissed because of a gruff or loud nature. We are more likely to be received well by others, more likely to be heard, when we use gentle ways and kind words.

Whenever I present this particular aspect of having a smart mouth in a seminar or retreat, I receive skeptical looks from the audience, many of whom have read books on assertiveness and getting what you want by speaking up and asking. There is nowhere in wisdom literature that suggests we not be assertive or forthcoming with our feelings, opinions, and instructions. Scripture does suggest that we never speak before we have assessed as much of the situation as we can, that we use a kind and gentle tone over a harsh and angry one, that we make our responses short and sweet—in other words, worth hearing. We can convey the same words in a variety of tones with a predictable variety of results.

For example, my children can request a glass of milk in two very different ways. For a gentle, sincere request I would walk to the ends of the earth to milk an insane cow, and for a loud, demanding request I generally suggest they pour their own glass of milk from the refrigerator.

Gentle speech makes your point in more ways than one.

5. Give wise instruction.

Studying the book of Proverbs gave me such good ammunition with my children. Nearly every day I wanted to quote to them Proverbs 1:8-9: "Listen, my son, to your father's instruction and do not forsake your mother's teaching. They will be a garland to grace your head and a chain to adorn your neck." This sounded pretty good. I can always use more scriptural backing to make my motherly points. Then I realized with a sickening thud that a large part of Solomon's exhortation was based on the fact that I would truly offer words of instruction that were worthy of hearing and heeding! As their instructor, I actually had to have something nourishing and wise to say!

What a blessing when I recognized Scripture is a ready-made instruction manual for parents, teachers, grandparents, and other significant adults to use with the children entrusted to them by God. (Proverbs 4 provides a wonderful model of instruction offered by a parent.)

We can be women of wise instruction when we carefully consider the person to whom we are speaking and prayerfully ask the Holy Spirit to help us recall relevant scripture or truth. Wisdom's promise resounds through Proverbs 3:6 once again, "In all your ways acknowledge him and he will make your paths straight." Hopefully you have already experienced that wonderful sense after a conversation that you were simply the mouthpiece for God's instruction, admonition, or encouragement. "A word aptly spoken is like apples of gold in settings of silver" (25:11).

I have had the privilege of encountering two people who embody this kind of wise instruction.

When my writing and speaking was in its infancy, I asked Dr. Jay Kesler, then president of Taylor University in Upland, Indiana, if I might have a valuable hour of his time to voice my vision so he could offer direction. During our visit, he sat quietly while I articulated the ideas brewing in my soul. With great care and patience he listened, and then he said, "You know, I've been praying about what you're saying the whole time you have been talking so that I could offer you wise counsel and direction." He prayed and really listened. What a gift! As he offered his insight and musings, I felt the conversation was anointed by the Holy Spirit, and I knew I was the blessed recipient of wise instruction.

My other wise counselor is my colleague Dr. Joan. With humor, unparalleled listening skills, and an ear for the "Third Voice" in every conversation, Joan has guided me through ideas and situations with great dexterity and wisdom. Whenever I have an idea for a project, seminar, or book, I go to Joan.

Joan attends with great interest. Then she does the most amazing thing. By asking a series of questions and making suggestions of options I might want to consider, she helps me get a clearer picture of my path and my plan. Although she rarely gives direct instruction, she guides in such wise ways as she lets me know she trusts the unfolding Holy Spirit in my own life. She makes me a better person because she values and believes in me. Wise instruction pays equal attention to the value of the person as well as to the value of the training.

6. Speak honestly.

Honesty ranks first place according to the number of proverbs given to its attention. Eugene Peterson sums it up graphically in *The Message*, Proverbs 12:22: "God can't stomach liars; he loves the company of those who keep their word." With good reason. People who are truthful clear the air (12:17 MSG), bring enduring fidelity to all situations (12:19), save souls (14:25), are a delight to those in charge (16:13; 22:11), stimulate affection and pleasure (24:26), and bring loving correction and clarity to behavior and situations (27:6).

Some of us have no trouble telling the truth! We can tell the truth about anything, anybody, anytime. The only trouble is we sometimes leave in our wake a string of wounded hearts and bleeding souls because of our harsh approach. On the other hand, some of us would be happy to tell the truth, except it might hurt somebody's feelings. It should come as no surprise that Proverbs 3:3 has advice for all of us when it comes to truth-telling: "Do not let kindness and truth leave you; bind them around your neck, write them on the tablet of your heart" (NASB). The wisdom of the sage is echoed years later when Paul admonishes the church at Ephesus, "God wants us to grow up, to know the whole truth and tell it in love—like Christ in everything" (Ephesians 4:15 MSG).

Truth and love in perfect balance. One way to look at how these two relate is through color. My favorite color is purple, so I see the continuum like this.

True blue is the space where there is all truth. Stark, raw, uncensored truth lives in this blue realm. The only problem here is if there is too much truth, I am decimated by the truth-teller.

Sympathetic love lives in the Valentine red space. This is the place where great compassion, nurture, and understanding dwell. The drawback on this end is there may be too much love and no accountability or cutting edge offered to me for my authentic and necessary growth to occur. Proverbs 12:1 says that "whoever loves discipline loves knowledge, but he who hates correction is stupid."

When someone speaks to me taking into consideration first my identity as a sister in Christ and my own particular temperament and circumstances, when she offers suggestions and feedback that truly benefit me and my contribution to God's kingdom, that person is giving me truth combined with love. She is speaking from the zone in which blue and red are combined—the purple zone. As a person of wisdom, I need to listen to what this sage advisor has to say.

Living in the purple zone will be easier if we start with ourselves. "We need to understand that our commitment to honesty, first and foremost, has to do with telling *ourselves* the truth—and telling the truth *about* ourselves."[1] When we practice telling the truth in love to ourselves, we can do it more easily with others. Because we neither over-inflate ourselves nor beat ourselves into the ground, we can be real, gentle, honest, and sometimes even humorous with others.

7. *Offer encouragement.*

Proverbs offers us at least four examples of what it means to be an encouraging woman.

Give a blessing to be a blessing. "Congenial conversation—what a pleasure! The right word at the right time—beautiful!" (Proverbs 15:23 MSG). Throughout the Old Testament, the blessing was the difference between life and death. To have a parent's blessing meant you could go forward in confidence—anyone who tried to defy you would find themselves in a pickle. The right word at the right time—such a gift to give, and such a treasure to receive.

Sweeten someone's soul with gratitude. "Pleasant words are a honeycomb, sweet to the soul and healing to the bones" (Proverbs 16:24). Some people have it, and some people have to cultivate it. My son, Grant, just naturally has it. He has the uncanny ability to thank me or hug me at just the right time in my day. He is so pleasant and polite and thoughtful and encouraging. When he says of his ham-and-cheese sandwich, "Thank you, Mommy, for this sandwich you made me," my heart is cleansed and whatever thought I was lost in evaporates as I drink in the wonderful elixir of someone appreciating what I have done. Expressing appreciation...

Heal someone's bones with love. Sometimes out of the blue, Madison will sigh with her head bowed over homework, "I love you, Mama," and I become completely refreshed, awash in the understanding that regardless of the kind of mommy I feel I am, I am loved, and those around me feel loved. Expressing appreciation and love are two highly encouraging ways for us to speak to others. Use them often and watch your world transform into the kingdom come on earth as it is in heaven. In this wild world we live in, people need to know they're loved and thought about in a positive way.

Give good news. "Like cold water to a weary soul is good news from a distant land" (Proverbs 25:25). Often we can be encouraged by a phone call, email, or a note that lets us know that someone far away is doing well, perhaps has recovered from surgery, has gotten a new job, or has had a prodigal return home. This proverb gives advice to stay in touch with people who we may not see all the time because of distance. In our society, so many families live far apart, and a good word from a close-yet-distant relative can make someone's day. It is always encouraging to know someone thought of us and that they are doing well.

We can be part of giving good news when we decide to speak positively instead of complaining. My friend Cheree observes, "The hardest thing to tame about my mouth is the urge to jump on the bandwagon when I'm in the midst of complainers. God has blessed me with so much. So why do I want to fit in with the crowd by finding fault with things? Too often women get in a little contest of who has the worst luck, and it's important to walk away from those conversations, rather than take part."

8. Be humble.

"Let another praise you, and not your own mouth; someone else, and not your own lips" (Proverbs 27:2). Les and Leslie Parrott, in their meditations of Proverbs for couples, call this "being your partner's publicist."[2] I have had the joy of knowing what they are talking about. One evening when out to dinner with my husband and two gentlemen he was entertaining for work, my husband broke into a lovely description of my work and ministry and what I was doing in its development. It was one of those moments when I fell in love with him all over again. He was proud of me, and he enjoyed what I was doing. And he was willing to lift me up in public! What a gift!

You can be a publicist for others. Don't give false flattery, for Proverbs speaks of the insincerity of the flatterer. Do give enthusiastic and heartfelt praise in front of others that uplifts and honors the one you're praising. When you do it as a surprise, so much the better! Let your children overhear you singing their accolades when you're talking with someone on the phone. Praise a friend in public. Give a colleague a big verbal pat on the back in front of others. Perhaps this is what King Lemuel's mother meant when she said, "She brings him good, not harm, all the days of her life" (Proverbs 31:12).

"If you have played the fool and exalted yourself, or if you have planned evil, clap your hand over your mouth!" (30:32). Don't try to make yourself look good; let other people do it for you. We will always come out shining when we let others tell of our strengths, good works, and insights. The temptation to brag ever so slightly is a sure path to enjoying our achievements less, not more, because of the bitter aftertaste of empty self-promotion. How much better to receive an accolade from the mouth of someone else and take genuine and humble pleasure from hearing the lovely words.

9. Make peace.

With one of the rich rewards of wisdom being peace, it's little wonder there are plenty of proverbs to guide us in the use of our tongue to bring peace to ourselves and to those around us. The proverbs that instruct in the ways of peace are actually about gossiping. A gossip is one who routinely destroys the possibility of peace in a situation because he or she is the wood that keeps the fires of strife burning (Proverbs 26:20), and they grab a passing dog by the ears (26:17). On the other hand, the one who puts a stop to offensive talk and hurtful conversation is a person of peace and love—and great wisdom (10:11-13).

Halting gossip when we encounter it is just as important as not gossiping in the first place.

Some gossip is benign; it is honestly not meant to hurt others. When I sit at lunch with a friend and say, "You won't believe what my husband just did," it's an effort to connect with the sisterhood, to be bonded with my friend in the joint incredulity of men. But I have taken a vow of faithfulness to my husband above all others, and I have broken that vow by telling something about him that he probably has not authorized. This may not seem like a big deal, except it has sown two bad seeds. The first is that my friend now has a new lens through which to look at my husband. Second, I have used my words to speak ill when in the same space in time and with the same breath, I could have spoken words that brought peace and goodness into the world.

Laura points out, "The hardest thing for me to tame about my mouth is wanting to join in the gossip going on around me at work. Sometimes it starts with factual information, but can lead to rumors and innuendo if not thwarted." Gossip can indeed be truthful, but is it helpful? Does it lead us to a healthy and loving place? It can degenerate quickly into unkind distortions of the truth.

Another seemingly innocent practice is bringing before your prayer group as a "prayer request" a choice morsel that you have discovered about someone you all know (Proverbs 26:22). "I just found out this week that Julie has been let go from her job for some questionable practices." Julie does indeed need prayer. But before we bring something like this before a group, we need to ask Julie directly if she wants others to know about her situation. If she doesn't, you can hit your knees all you want on your own for intercession. If she does, maybe she can make a written request to the group or be more directly involved in asking for prayer. No matter how well-intentioned our motive when engaging in this practice, it is never right to bring up someone else's need to a group when we have not been confirmed to do so. It is gossip.

These are two ways that gossip just slips out of our mouths, and we don't really mean to injure someone in the process. Other types of gossip are more overt and intended for hurt and division.

As justified as we might feel when someone has hurt us, or when we feel someone is clearly on the wrong side of an issue and we need to gather support, the way of wisdom commands that we keep our mouths quiet until we are truly searching for peace. Any division we have with someone is to be taken up directly with that person. A woman at a seminar once told me her

Bible-study group was having a horrific struggle between the women who were staying home with their children and those who were working outside the home. She once walked into a room with several members huddled around one particular member, who was strenuously speaking against one of the other members who was not present. The absent member was in the "enemy camp," and the speaking member was seeking to gather support for her position against her sister in Christ. I have learned through various encounters like this on a variety of topics that God is less interested where we come down on an issue than how we treat others in the discussion.

Jesus didn't say we had to all agree on topics, but He was praying for our unity in spirit and in love (John 17:21-23).

Halting gossip when we encounter it is just as important as not gossiping in the first place. Proverbs offers two ways for us to do this. "Gossips can't keep secrets, so never confide in blabber-mouths" (20:19 MSG). Don't give confirmed gossips material to spread. Give them no logs for their fires. "You'll find wisdom on the lips of a person of insight, but the shortsighted needs a slap in the face" (10:13 MSG). While I don't advocate we physically slap the offending gossip, I do suggest we take a proactive stance to calling the foolishness of the gossip's behavior as we see it. In private and with love, of course.

When it comes to gossip and peacemaking, Christ offered a wise and time-tested rule that has never failed yet: "Here is a simple, rule-of-thumb guide for behavior: Ask yourself what you want people to do for you, then grab the initiative and do it for them. Add up God's Law and Prophets and this is what you get" (Matthew 7:12 MSG).

My internet tea buddy, Denise, shared with me two exam-ples from her own life of women who have learned to harness this habit. "Believe it or not, my 17-year-old daughter comes to mind when I think of an example of wise speech. She does not participate in gossip or trashing of 'friends.' She is weary of many of her classmates because of the habit of so many to talk about those who are not present. She never adds to news I share about difficulties others are having…even when she has what could be thought to be 'the scoop' on others. She keeps prayer requests silent and private. She shares what truly will benefit others and not harm them.

"My grandmother, now deceased, was another example for me. She never said an unkind word about anyone. She comes to mind when I have a choice before me to share a prayer request that has private details with a mutual friend or not at all.…"

As one of my favorite modern-day sages, Mary Englebreit, quoted in her 1999 Proverbial Calendar for the month of March—

> There's so much good in the worst of us
> And so much bad in the best of us
> It ill behooves any of us
> To talk about the rest of us.

10. Be discreet.

Being crass or vulgar is one sure way to get people's attention.

Teenagers do it all the time because it makes the grownups sit up and take notice. Sometimes we use coarse or gross language because we just "want to get the point across." But the point we end up making could very well be different than the point we intended to make!

Ephesians 5:4 counsels, "Nor should there be obscenity, foolish talk or coarse joking, which are out of place, but rather thanksgiving." My friend Becky calls it having a "potty mouth," and she believes this is one of the hardest areas in which to maintain a smart mouth. Some of us talk coarsely because it's what we did before we began the transformation into the likeness of Jesus. Some of us talk this way because our families did when we were growing up. Some of us talk this way because we just get fed up with trying to be good all of the time! Whatever the reason, it evokes a startling image in Proverbs 11:22: "Like a gold ring in a pig's snout is a beautiful woman who shows no discretion." Beauty is not just physical. We were all meant to be beautiful. But we'll end up looking as foolish as a pig wearing jewelry if we aren't discreet in the way we speak.

11. Confess wisely.

You will never succeed in life if you try to hide your sins. Confess them and give them up; then God will show you mercy (Proverbs 28:13). When you have done something that needs confessing, go directly to the person whom your transgression has offended. Make peace; accept forgiveness. One of my favorite images of confession is "run to the roar." When a group of lions is stalking prey, they designate one lion to stand up and roar, hopefully scaring the prey so it runs into the circle of lions hidden in waiting. If the prey will run to the roar, they are less likely to be ensnared by the hunters. In the same way, don't wait for your sin to come looking for you. When you know you need to confess, do it quickly and appropriately.

Appropriate confession means you involve only the parties who really need to know. Wise confession means a truthful accounting of wrong, apology for the consequences, an offer to make things right, and then turning from the transgression in the future. To give up the sin means to free yourself from the guilt and not to repeat the practice in the future.

Wise confession can also live as wise self-disclosure. Self-disclosure is telling something to someone that they don't already know about you. Wise women know when to say things, to whom they should say them, and to what degree they should reveal themselves. Several factors determine wise disclosure.

Your temperament. By nature some of us are more open with everything that is going on with us. Some of us are more reserved. Figure out where your comfort zone is and move in and out of this zone as you sense is appropriate.

Your culture. You may be from an ethnic, economic, or family culture that feels it's better to "play things close to the vest" or keep more information to yourself. You may be from a culture that "lets it all hang out." How much you choose to self-disclose is initially influenced by this culture, and wise women know they should always think critically about what's best for them.

Your listeners. Your degree of self-disclosure is definitely dependent on your listeners. The context of your conversation has a great deal to say about how much you want or should tell the receivers of your information. An intimate gathering of people you trust will bring out different information than when you're with a party of people you are just getting acquainted with. While this sounds obvious, you may have been exposed to someone who has trouble distinguishing the sometimes subtle differences with results that range from mildly uncomfortable to downright embarrassing or inappropriate.

Your topic. You may feel very comfortable talking about family matters with nearly everyone, but financial topics are definitely off-limits. You get to decide. You are in charge. Avoid being influenced to speak about topics you don't wish to speak about simply because the rest of the conversation leans that way. A wise woman knows who she is, what her limits are, and how she will feel about herself if those limits are violated.

Wise confession comes from a woman who is in control of her mouth, her personal preferences, and her appropriate boundaries.

12. *Keep it shut!*

Eleven of the "Dynamic Dozen" have to do with actually speaking. But there is one more very important piece of advice. Never underestimate the power of silence: "A man of knowledge uses words with restraint, and a man of understanding is even-tempered. Even a fool is thought wise if he keeps silent, and discerning if he holds his tongue" (Proverbs 17:27-28). As my wise and clever friend Libby quips, "I need to remember that every thought traveling through my mind does not need to exit my mouth!"

Being quiet gives us more opportunity to actually listen. Throughout the book of Proverbs we are encouraged to embrace instruction (1:8), pay attention to experienced teachers (4:1), walk with the wise (13:20), seek counsel and sound advice (15:22), seek knowledge with our ears (18:15), and listen to the law (28:9). Perhaps this is why some have observed that we each have one mouth and two ears.

Careful listening brings special benefits to our lives. These include successful plans, increased wisdom, gaining complete information, and prayers that are heard and honored. The more we listen to and apply the guidance of wise counsel, the deeper and firmer our relationship grows with Lady Wisdom.

Being quiet can keep us out of trouble. When we take the time to be quiet, we have a chance to truly weigh the benefits and costs of what we intend to say. "When in doubt, don't" is a wonderful piece of folk advice I often use (although probably not often enough) when it comes to speaking or not. Any of us can look over our lives and rue the idiotic, cruel, misguided, or silly things we have said. This piece of wisdom needn't take a lifetime to learn. If we learn and model for younger women this delicate and lovely characteristic, many tears and sleepless nights can be avoided. An anonymous quote I received by email said, "While we're learning to have a smart mouth, let's also train it to be quiet when the time is right."

Muscle Control

Which pounds are the hardest to take and keep off? The last ones just before you hit the target! Anyone who has dieted or trained will tell you the final few are the hardest to control. It's all the extra stuff we put into our mouths and the exercise we skip that makes the biggest difference. Getting into spiritual shape is similar. There is always going to be something that is the biggest challenge in maintaining optimum spiritual fitness. For most of us it has to do with what comes out of our mouths and the control we fail to exercise over our words.

As noted at the beginning of this chapter, the tongue is a pretty unruly creature. Usually when I teach this at seminars, women seem to sink lower and lower in their chairs, burdened by the impossible load of taming the tongue. James 3:8 gives insight into a great comfort about our speech: "No man can tame the tongue. It is a restless evil, full of deadly poison." At first blush this doesn't look much like encouragement, but the statement begs the question, "Well, who can?" Thanks be to God for the powerful gift of the Holy Spirit who can tame anything woman cannot! By the indwelling of and constant reliance on the Holy Spirit, we can count on our tongues serving us well and keeping us out of trouble.

Cut the fat out of your spiritual diet. Start with one area of speech at a time, conquer it with the help of the Holy Spirit, and move to the next one. Exercise control over your tongue and experience the best spiritual shape of your walk with God!

GOING DEEPER

Warm-up: As you feel comfortable, tell about a time when you said something really dumb.

1. Review the "Dynamic Dozen" ways to have a smart mouth. What do each of these mean to you on an everyday basis? Give examples of people you know who do any of these well. What impact has that person's wise speech had on you?

2 Which one of these 12 is the easiest way for you to be a woman of wise speech? How can you apply it more to your life?

3. Which one of these 12 is the most difficult area for you as a woman of wise speech? What needs to happen in your life for it to become more evident?

4. What does it mean to apply each of these areas to your intrapersonal communication or how you speak and listen to yourself?

5. Is there a connection between how well you communicate with yourself and how well you communicate with others? Explain.

6. What are the benefits of wise listening?
   a. Proverbs 15:22—
   b. Proverbs 13:20—
   c. Proverbs 18:17—
   d. Proverbs 28:9—

7. Who have been the wise instructors in your life? Write them a note or call them and tell them how they have influenced you in your spiritual growth.

8. Precisely around the topic of our tongue Proverbs 3:5-6 starts to make the most sense: "Trust in the LORD with all your heart and lean not on your own understanding." How could using this passage aid you in becoming more wise with your communication?

9. Read James 3:3-12 and 3:17-18. What is our hope as we seek to be wise in this arena?

10. Benjamin Franklin was renowned for his focus on positive character traits. He kept a series of traits foremost in his mind by focusing on one each week. Make a deck of twelve 3 x 5 cards, each with a separate item from the Dynamic Dozen. Start week one with the first trait. Keep the card visible wherever you are most likely to see it to be reminded of that week's trait. On week two, go to the next card. By the time the year is through, you will have been through your deck at least four times, and you will have much wiser speech. If you live with a family or you have coworkers who would like to participate in this exercise with you, put a poster up weekly of the trait and see what happens! Will you do this?

Assignment for this week: For a couple days, keep a "smart mouth" journal. Note wise and unwise speech in yourself. Consistently turn over this area of your life to the guidance of the Holy Spirit.

5

THE SERVICE ADVANTAGE

Who is wise and understanding among you? Let him show it by his good life, by deeds done in the humility that comes from wisdom.

JAMES 3:13

The noblest service comes from nameless hands, and the best servant does his work unseen.

OLIVER WENDELL HOLMES

The woman is in absolute anguish. She has fallen in love and has run away trying to make sense of the immense conflict between her devotion to God and her womanly instincts. As is the wise thing to do, she seeks counsel from a trusted advisor, from someone who knows her very well and walks in the Spirit of God. As the conversation unfolds and the emerging romance love is revealed, the Reverend Mother says to the distressed Maria, "You have a great capacity to love. What we must find out is how God wants you to spend your love."

"But I've pledged my life to God. I've pledged my life to His service," Maria laments.

"My daughter, if you love this man, it doesn't mean you love God less."

And at this turning point in Rogers and Hammerstein's 1965 classic *The Sound of Music*, Maria is blessed with the permission to meld her heart's longing with her profound desire to remain true to the service of God. She has discovered, with the help of an insightful and loving friend, that the two desires are best understood as sisters, not distant cousins.

The wise woman in this wild world knows that service is not something she does, it is something she is. Service is a mind-set that informs everything we do, not a task to be checked off the to-do list. To grasp this distinction takes us a long way in erasing some of the common objections as to why we "really can't serve right now." Remember, wisdom has more to do with character than performance. Performance can have a faulty, external motive, while pure character produces pure results.

The True Nature of Service

Service comes out of living in tune with your essence. Your essence is best described as your real and individual nature. Essential oils give plants their characteristic odors. Likewise your essence is your own particluar set of foundational characteristics, interests, and gifts. This essence is first found in being grounded with God, then is shown in whatever nature you feel is genuine and authentic in you.

True service also comes from having cultivated a sense of gratitude and contentment. James calls it "the humility that comes from wisdom" (James 3:13). Why does wisdom produce humility? Because the truly wise woman is walking humbly with her God. She maintains a healthy perspective of who she is and who God is. This humility is characterized by the security a woman finds when she is supremely grateful for her relationship with God and content in the moment-by-moment gift of God's presence.

That is one reason service is such a challenge. It is sometimes hard work to cultivate gratitude and contentment. Often it boils down to sheer willpower and practice. When we are concerned with our own gain, it is spiritually impossible to allow service to flow from our hearts toward God and those we love.

As I've mentioned, in my younger days my focus was on professional success. I was busy making my place in the world. I needed to be noticed and really didn't have time to waste on efforts that weren't going to be applauded or recognized. But I could never be an authentic servant with that mind-set. I was always looking for what I would get out of the service opportunity. What I didn't realize is that I didn't need to carve out my niche. "These are the keys to servanthood. If we're confident of our place in God's family, we don't have to make a name for ourselves. If we're assured that we come from God and are called by God, we can be content to be invisible. If we are certain that our future lies with God, we don't have to exalt ourselves for our ultimate exaltation is already accomplished in Jesus Christ."[1]

Serving has a way of completely altering our lives because it changes us in two important ways. First, Proverbs gives us a beautiful promise to ponder: "Your own soul is nourished when you are kind" (11:17 TLB). When we feed the goodness in our hearts by having and sharing a spirit of generosity, we starve the negative forces inside. When we are kind, our soul feeds on that kindness and gets stronger, more fortified for more genuine service. Darkness subsides as light appears. Our own soul is nourished as we feel more in tune with answering God's call and living our purpose.

Second, our lives are changed because Christ knew exactly what He was talking about when He said, "Ask yourself what you want people to do for you; then grab the initiative and do it for them!" (Luke 6:31 MSG). This suggests we use the power of self-awareness to know what we want and need. Then we are able to use the power of initiative to make the world a better place, in Jesus' name. Christ encourages us to be dynamically empowered, not just sitting around waiting for something to happen.

Authentic Service

One way to assess your true desire for service and in what area is what seems to surface over and over again as a passion or point of keen interest in your life. When you get to the basics of who you are, true and fitting ways to serve consistently come to your heart.

Becky highlights that God makes this point with us over time. "The one call that keeps coming over and over again in so many big and little ways is my role in mission leadership. About 20 years ago, I visited a former inner city Presbyterian Church. Upon entering the unused and rundown sanctuary, I wept at the utter uselessness of it. To see a boarded up, formerly beautiful house of God just ripped at my very soul. Since then, I have worked on and off to bring mission to the people where *they* are—not where *we* are. It has not always been easy, but it has always been necessary. I'm still in the midst of this. It will not go away and the job is even bigger now. Mother Teresa said, 'Find your own Calcutta.' This is what I am doing."

Becky has sought to keep her heart as aligned with God as possible. She seeks to truly know who she *is*, so she can know what she should truly *do*.

Real Life Blocks to Service

Even when our hearts are more in tune with God's call to service, we may have a few more questions.

With my life as overloaded as it already is, how am I going to find time to serve? The Original Wise Woman stretched out her hands to the poor and the needy. However, sometimes we can't get to the food pantry or the homeless shelter. With the over-time we're putting in or the carpools we're driving, we can't always minister to the overtly poor and needy. Yet we must never make the mistake of thinking the poor and the needy refer only to those in economic poverty. The woman in the next cubicle may be poor in spirit; perhaps she is just aching for a good word. Your husband or significant other needs a safe place to turn at the end of the day. Your child feels poorly for the failed math test, or your neighbor needs an invitation to come to your house for chili sometime during the winter. Look for the small and obvious needs right under your own nose, and let your Spirit-led intuition tell you what to do.

What do I have to offer the world? I'm only an accountant...or a mother...or a high school graduate...or a seamstress...or a shut-in. Ephesians 2:10 tells us we were created for good works that God established before we were born! The center of your service is wherever you are, and God laid it all out for you from the beginning of time while He was creating, with Wisdom by His side, and rejoicing over you! (Proverbs 8:31). So each moment is a moment of service, each exchange is in God's name, every loving action builds the kingdom of God.

If I am supposed to die to myself and take up my cross, isn't it inappropriate to do what I like to do as a way of serving? There is a well-kept secret about service: You can actually enjoy it! It's okay to do something you feel called to do and, conversely, leave off your platter the things you don't feel an authentic Spirit-filled tug to do. Let's be honest. You may start a project that you initially thought you could squeeze into your schedule or learn to love, but at some point the grumpies took over and you asked yourself, "Why did I let them talk me into this?"

> *When we serve from our essence, from our call, we do it happily with anticipation and a detachment from the outcome or reward.*

So be creative in finding out what you like to do. Take your time in sorting through opportunities. Leave on the shelf the things you feel you ought to do and the things you cannot do. Nobody wants to be around someone they look to for benevolence only to find a snarling, disgruntled "helper."

When you look into the face of the Almighty early every day and ask, "Where do You want me to go today?" you set the stage for and enable an amazing and sometimes mysterious series of opportunities and events. Every day becomes an adventure in which we lose ourselves and keep our eyes focused on the next enterprise presented by our loving heavenly Parent. When we serve from our essence, from our call, we do it happily with anticipation and a detachment from the outcome or reward.

Is my small service offering really going to make a difference anyway? Even when we are at peace with submitting to Christ's direction and are genuinely serving out of love, gratitude, and our essence, we can be overwhelmed by the world of need we face every day. I don't know about you, but often as I watch CNN or MSNBC, I am once again astounded by the immense suffering of the hungry, the homeless, the oppressed, and the hopeless. What good does my life of service do to really change the world? In those moments I have to remember that the breakfast I give my kids means the world to them and the clothes I clean out of my closet to take to church allows a teenager to go to school dressed rather than dropping out for lack of covering. What you feel is a pitiful little offering may save someone's life. That's the beauty and mystery of partnering with God!

What if I get burned out? What if we become swamped by the service we offer? We may overextend, and people may expect too much of us. Proverbs 3:27 offers wise advice as we make decisions on how much to extend ourselves: "Do not withhold good from those who deserve it, when it is in your power to act." The key phrase here is "when it is in your power to act."

We are each bestowed with gifts and graces, but not any of us has them all! We are each given 24 hours a day. And nobody I know has yet found a way to be two places at the same time!

When we feel overwhelmed, it's time to stop and ask, "What is on my plate? How did it get there? Are there any unhealthy motives for anything I'm doing?" Whenever you are feeling trapped, smothered, or angered by service, decide to let go of whatever motive and activity has you snared. Keeping Paul's advice to "make the most of every opportunity" (Ephesians 5:16) steadily before your eyes will go a long way in helping you see where you can serve. In *Sound of Music*, the Reverend Mother told Maria at the end of their conversation, "You have to live the life you were born to live."

A "SERVICE" TREASURE HUNT

How likely are you to see service as something you are rather than something you do? Use the following scale in responding to each statement:

5=always   4=often   3=sometimes   2=rarely   1=never

_____ 1. I am too busy to serve.

_____ 2. I don't have anything of real value to offer because I don't have any special titles, degrees, skills, or talents.

_____ 3. I believe that if you are enjoying what you are doing, it's not really the kind of service God expects.

_____ 4. I don't see that anything I can do will make a difference.

_____ 5. I'm afraid I'll get overloaded and burned out.

Unlike the other Treasure Hunts in this book, this time you are trying to achieve a low score. The lower your score the more you understand that service is anywhere you are. You don't feel the need to seek out a lot of extracurricular opportunities that don't fit into your lifestyle or schedule. You don't place undue demands on yourself because you know that service is an attitude and can be accomplished in any moment, at any place, with any one. If you have a high score on this scale, what can you do to discover the opportunities to serve today?

The Unseen Servant

We can never underestimate the power of the support we bring to others who are serving. We can take vicarious satisfaction in the service of others whom we are serving behind the scenes. Our covert service to them allows them to render overt service to others.

A dear, indirect service role model for me is my mother. Having served directly for many years as a public school teacher and a mental-health professional, my mother answered the call to a less public service role when my husband and I both worked in a church when my son was a toddler. She daily took care of Grant and ensured that he had an extraordinary childhood. My husband and I were enabled to directly serve in the church by her indirect service. She was also living proof that we can enjoy the service to which God has called us. With regularity she would tell people, "It's the best job I've ever had!" And my son was highly blessed, as well.

Another powerful and effective example of indirect service comes from Jill:

> As a mom, I am privileged to be part of a powerful prayer group called "Moms in Touch." Our group meets weekly to pray for our school-aged children, the teachers, and the public school they attend. We are encouraged as we see God move on behalf

of our humble prayers, and our children are enlightened as they see our trust in God. I took Christmas cookies, baked by all the local moms who pray, into my daughter's school this past December. My heart was touched as I entered the teacher's lounge, and they all turned to me and asked, "Are these from the moms who pray for us? Thank you *so much* for all you do!"

Laura says she and her family support a husband–wife missionary team that ministers to youth. She quips, "They do the 'work,' and we chip in the money."

You may know women like Linda's mother. You may very well *be* a woman like Linda's mother. "My mother is a wonderful 'behind the scenes' person. She is the individual who helps cook and clean up after enormous fellowship dinners. It isn't important to her that others know what she has done. As a matter of fact, her preference would always be to go unnoticed. However, she uses her time and gifts and enjoys the fellowship of helping in some of the less glamorous jobs."

Behind-the-scenes servants often do their work quietly and without calling attention to themselves. Because service is something they are instead of something they do, they don't always recognize that they are doing anything out of the ordinary, and they don't want to be overtly recognized. Becky shared her experience as a behind-the-scenes servant:

> In the late 1980s, I was the chair of the Christmas Benevolence project at my church. Planning and preparations take an entire year involving scores of volunteers who serve hundreds of individuals at Christmastime. I was in my mid-thirties with three grade-school children and was doing the huge job of juggling husband, kids, school PTO president, and church. One of the television stations wanted to come and film the actual day we

delivered everything to the families in the community. Delivery is a wonderful day of total and mass confusion, but somehow it always works. The reporter wanted to interview me on camera. I felt the pictures were much more important than anything I could say, so I declined. I had several people tell me I was wrong not to "toot" the church's horn, but I still believe that I made the right decision.

Susan, a health-care provider, witnessed firsthand the life-changing dynamic of the unseen servant as she observed hospice care:

I saw the ministry of hospice care by the nurses and volunteers as a behind-the-scenes role. On the outside the work was seen as a healthcare service, but behind the closed doors of a patient's room, by the bedside, the nurse or volunteer was often listening to the heartfelt pain of the patient as he or she struggled with the issues related to living until death. So often I felt the nurse and patient relationship became one of the most intimate experiences of that patient's life. Many times we saw people living in rural areas of Indiana, underprivileged and often less educated. No one will ever know what a ministry this work can be unless they are called to live it. It had so much impact on my maturity, thinking, and wisdom regarding the true meaning of life and what is truly of value. It sure allowed me a privileged insight into the walk toward the next life on a very uncertain road at times. It helped me to experience God and His fullness of forgiveness and love.

What can you do to develop a life of service? Make a game with yourself to see how many wonderful things you can find to do in secret, and then do them. Service is a way of life, not an isolated project. Little things done in private can make a big difference in the big picture.

GOING DEEPER

Warm-up: What have you done in the last month that left you feeling really good?

1. Respond to the statement, "Service is not something you do, it's something you are." How does this tie into the importance of having a good sense of your essence or call?

2. Describe a time you felt gratitude or contentment in your life. What did it prompt you to do?

3. "A kind man benefits himself" (Proverbs 11:17). Describe a time when this happened to you. Write a poem or paint a picture that illustrates this proverb.

4. What can you do to "do to others as you would have them do to you"?

5. Can you love your neighbor if you do not love yourself? Please explain.

6. Read Proverbs 11:25. What does this have to say about authentic service?

7. What are some roadblocks to your service?

8. Who are the poor and needy in your life? How can you help them?

9. Are you more in a direct service mode or an indirect service mode at this point in your life? How do you feel about that?

10. Consider this quote from Mother Teresa: "Don't look for spectacular actions. What is important is the gift of yourselves. It is the degree of love you insert in your deed." How does this impact the way

you see yourself as "service"? In the upcoming week, where will you have opportunities to serve?

Assignment for this week: Live in the moment with love, gratitude, and contentment. As much as possible, put aside heavy-duty agendas and see what opportunities for service present themselves as you seek to do deeds in the humility that comes from wisdom.

6

WISE LAUGHTER

She is clothed with strength and dignity; she can laugh at the days to come.

PROVERBS 31:25

It is pleasing to God whenever you rejoice or laugh from the bottom of your heart.

MARTIN LUTHER

The doctor says there's a little spot she wants me to have checked out by a specialist. I didn't really want to tell you until you got home, but I guess I just had to let you know." My husband spoke those words to me on the Sunday of a long weekend when I was away with two girlfriends on a little jaunt to Florida. He was in his Indiana hometown with our two kids, and it was the first time since Friday that we had connected. As my pounding heart and churning stomach tried to grasp what he was telling me, the worst scenes budded then came into full bloom in my racing mind. Not only was my heart sick over the thought of losing my soul mate, my beloved, I also realized what a poor steward I had been with my resources on many levels.

Did I know where our finances stood? Had I built the kind of relationship with my kids that could stand the test of me being their only parent? Did my husband know beyond any doubt how truly special and dear he was to me? Was the house in good repair? Had I made wise investments into my support system in case I now needed to draw on the interest? Had I spent my time discerning my path, my mission, that would transcend the role of wife and at the same time provide for my family? Was my own faith strong enough to weather this storm? I'll tell you one thing, I didn't feel strong and dignified...nor was I laughing.

It is said of the Original Wise Woman that she could laugh at the days to come. She could laugh because she was a good steward. She took care of the clothing in her home. She kept herself strong. She made sure her family was gainfully occupied. She invested the money she made from her entrepreneurial efforts.

God's Economy

Good stewardship is one way God laughs with and through us as His ends are accomplished through us by the outpouring of His provision and our prudent usage. Second Corinthians 9:8 gives a radical accounting of God's economy: "God is able to make all grace abound to you, so that in all things at all times, having all that you need, you will abound in every good work." This does not hint that perhaps if God is in a good mood, or if I've been a particularly good girl that maybe God will give me a tad of grace to halfway do a job that may benefit someone. The word "abound" is used twice and "all" is used four times! This passage gushes with possibility if we learn how to tap into God's accounts and use well what we find available to us on a constant basis. It's no accident that one of the most enduring and often sung songs of the Christian faith is the Doxology (Praise God from whom all blessings flow...). We are meant to understand that the blessings do indeed flow!

A wise woman in a wild world is the consummate steward. She understands the spiritual laws in God's economy:

1. The more you appreciate what you have, the more you have.

2. The more you use what you've got, the more you've got.

3. The more you care for and cultivate what has been given to you, the more will come your way.

4. The more joy and satisfaction you bring to your world, the more you bring to yourself.

5. The more you trust in God to guide you, the more you feel that guidance.

Stewardship is an issue of trust.

In what ways do wise women allow God to laugh through them as they trust in Him for protection and provision?

Quality Control

"She selects wool and flax and works with eager hands" (Proverbs 31:13). As part of our stewardship, we make sure we have the very best materials to work with to create the best quality product we can. Because we choose good resources, we can be excited about our work and what we produce. If part of our call involves working with our hands in a craft, we use the best materials we can find to ensure that our product can be a lovely example of fine raw materials encountering the Master's touch. If our call requires training, we need to get the best we possibly can to make the most of what we've been given to work with. If our products are intangible, such as running a household, we should secure the best advice and input on making it all it can be.

Household Administration

Wise women take administration seriously. We stay ahead of the game with our family. We anticipate when they need to eat and prepare for this. The Original Wise Woman also had servant girls in her household (oh, *that's* how she got so much done!) and saw to it that they had work to keep them gainfully busy, which aided in the overall management of the home. Today we have dishwashers, washing machines, dryers, and ovens to act as our servants. One of our tasks may be to see that our machines are all properly and effectively used. And when it comes to cleaning, I don't personally feel the need to do all of the household chores myself, but I am a good steward of my family's energy when it comes time to straighten up the house.

A wise woman "watches over the affairs of her household" (31:27). As part of the domestic administration of a household, a wise woman guarantees that her children are occupied. Today we oversee homework, sign permission slips, teach the children how to launder their own sports uniforms, and keep the family calendar under control. We may also offer advice to lovelorn teenagers and heartbroken ex-best friends.

As wise household stewards, we are the central nervous system of the family. Our own physical central nervous system picks up signals from our limbs and senses and sends messages to the brain, which then gives instructions for what to perceive and how to respond. The central nervous system of the family keeps lots of signals straight and makes recommendations for interpreting the world and responding to all that comes into the lives of each person in our household.

Physical Management

A wise woman keeps herself in good shape. "Her arms are strong for her task" (Proverbs 31:17). This physical strengthening helps women to most efficiently carry out tasks, to oversee investments, and to effectively manage the entire household. What a relief in our beautiful-body-conscious society! So often we are obsessed with staying in good form or are depressed when we don't feel we measure up. The amount of exercise we need is the amount it takes to keep us in optimum shape to carry out our mission. The focus is on our health, not our physique.

And yet, we also exhibit stewardship over our appearance. Physical presentation is congruent with who we know ourselves to be as God's gift to family and community. Whatever your purpose, dress appropriately, comfortably, and in a way that is authentic with your personality. Look deeply into your motives for dressing and appearance. Make them as pure as possible, then dress to your strengths and God's glory.

Wise women eat well, stay active, and use the strength gathered from stewardship to make a positive impact.

Wise women eat well, stay active, and use the strength gathered from stewardship to make the positive impact on the world that God has given them to make.

Internal Affairs

Proverbs 31:25 mentions two other wardrobe items Wisdom wears regularly: "She is clothed with strength and dignity." Even more important than what we array our bodies in, is the internal raiment we choose from the wardrobe of characteristics. Keeping our spiritual clothing clean and in good repair will do more to keep us beautiful and attractive than any spa treatments and makeup lessons.

"Gray Matter" Matters

Our minds are very powerful resources. This is why Jesus said, "Watch out that no one deceives you" (Matthew 24:4). Paul reminds us "the peace of God, which transcends all understanding, will guard your hearts and your minds in Christ Jesus." He then goes on to give a wonderful list of what we want to keep our minds occupied with that will help in that guarding:

> Finally, brothers, whatever is true, whatever is noble, whatever is right, whatever is pure, whatever is lovely, whatever is admirable—if anything is excellent or praiseworthy—think about such things. Whatever you have learned or received or heard from me, or seen in me—put it into practice. And the God of peace will be with you (Philippians 4:8-9).

A wise woman is also a critical thinker. This is not the same as having a critical spirit. One builds up; the other tears down. A wise woman uses these interpersonal and intrapersonal skills:

1. She thinks for herself and is not easily manipulated by others.

2. She recognizes her own perspectives and can articulate from where her beliefs have come.

3. She evaluates the sender of the message, the vehicle of the message, and the motivation of the sender.

4. She realizes that we all believe ourselves to be the center of the universe at one point or another, and she works to overcome this egocentrism.

5. She considers all available information when working on a problem or making a decision.

6. She is a good questioner, seeking to get to the heart of a matter.

7. She welcomes the good questions of others, knowing this helps to clarify her thinking. She is not defensive, confused, or intimidated.

Wise, critically thinking women are wary of advertising, bandwagons, and anyone who tells them they should think or do something because "that's the way we have always thought about it or done it."

When you are a good steward of your mind, you are a supremely wise woman.

Business as Usual

The Original Wise Woman was an entrepreneur making full use of the gifts God had given her to bring financial support to her family. She was a speculator—looking at and buying land—and using the money she earned to reinvest in a field. She was a smart businesswoman as she kept her eye on the marketplace and knew the value of everything she made (Proverbs 31:18). Her esteem of her work kept her energized to work late into the night. She loved to work and took pleasure in providing products that would benefit the community and enrich her family.

The gifts we bring to this world as workers in an organization, workers who are never paid monetarily, or workers who are self-employed are simply more resources to be managed with wisdom. We need to keep an eye on the value of our products and services so we are adequately compensated, while not over-inflating our worth and damaging our ability to minister in the community. When we are doing what we love and feel we are earning a fair wage or return on our efforts, we find energy to work hours the normal, unmotivated worker would not consider. It flows from who we are and gives us a God-given grace we extend to others.

Good stewardship of the finances means we also weigh the costs and potential benefits of using our resources. Jesus pointed out to His listeners in Luke 14:28-30 that they wisely counted the cost before starting certain projects. He commended them for doing the same thing in their spiritual lives, as well.

Five of the wisest women in the New Testament are highlighted in Matthew 25:1-8. They are the wise virgins who conserved the oil in their lamps while waiting for the bridegroom. They knew when to spend their resources and when to safeguard their resources. They are called "wise" three times in the space of just seven verses.

The Stuff of Life

A wise woman's stewardship encompasses her household possessions. She knows good stewardship means taking care of what she has, such as keeping her clothes in good repair. When you provide good maintenance, you spend less money in the long run and prevent costly repairs. Karen regularly wears clothing she has had for over a decade. The secret to their longevity? She buys classic clothing that is well made, and she cares for her clothing with tenderness and attention. Betty provides consistent and complete maintenance for her cars. She is able to drive a car long after it has been paid for, freeing up money in the budget for other things while she has good, dependable transportation for years. When possible, the optimum combination for stewardship of our material things is to purchase the best we possibly can, and then ensure good condition through routine and tender care.

A true test of stewardship is what we do when resources are scarce. Sometimes we have to exhibit the faith of Christ in the feeding of the multitudes. We must trust in God's ability to produce the impossible through our willingness to lay our seemingly meager assets in His hands. God seems to delight in people of trust as He makes a memorable example of their faith. Patsy Clairmont remembers,

> My mom could do anything, especially with her hands. Organize, customize or economize, she could do it all. She could take a shack and transform it into a cottage. She could take a chicken and concoct a feast, and she could take a nickel and create a bankroll. I don't know how she did what she did with what she had, but perhaps growing up in a large family on a farm, living through the Depression, and marrying a milkman

gave her opportunity to be creative, versatile, resourceful and industrious.[1]

A profoundly wise way to be a good steward with your things is to lighten up. As I like to say, "Don't get 'stuffed' to death." How much time do we really spend on upkeep, sorting, pushing through piles, and telling ourselves we'll take care of it later? The rule we have in our house is if you haven't worn it, played with it, used it, or in any other way enjoyed or touched it in a year, it's out of the house. We lighten up on a regular basis by clearing away the items we don't want or need. Get your stuff in a pile, take that pile to the trash or to charity, and then quell the impulse to get more. You'll feel much lighter.

Time Will Tell

The stewardship of your time is one of the most telling ways of measuring your trust. When you are "doing less in a day but doing it with more passion, purpose, and power" (see Industrial Revolution in Chapter 3), and you are grounded in your basics, you've gone a long way in assuring that you are a good steward of the 24 hours of each day God has given you. You will not make promises of your resources that are off your path. Being fully assured that God is in control of every situation and God has created an answer for every need, you are free, knowing that it is someone else's mission to teach Sunday school, head the PTO, sew for the homeless shelter downtown, or raise money for the new organ.

But sometimes, for a variety of well-meaning reasons, we say yes to a task or commitment we really wish we had said no to. Proverbs offers very helpful coaching for those who find themselves caught in the poor stewardship of their promises and pledges. Go humbly to those to whom you made the pledge and extract yourself as quickly and thoroughly from the pledge as possible. In this way you "free yourself, like a gazelle from the hand of the hunter, like a bird from the snare of the fowler" (Proverbs 6:5).

Good stewardship of time is summed up in a provocative story I received from a friend. Normally I delete forwarded emails, but this is one I'm glad I read. The insightful, anonymous writer was right on target.

It seems Satan held a convention with all of his evil angels. They were all bemoaning the fact that they can't keep Christians from reading their Bibles, going to church, or holding certain values. But Satan had a plan nonetheless. If they could keep Christians so busy that they couldn't pursue an authentic relationship with God, they could win a great share in the battle.

Satan instructed his minions to keep humans busy in the nonessentials of life. He told them to get humans to spend, spend, spend, then borrow, borrow, borrow. To top that off, humans should be drawn to work long hours, keeping parents away from their children and fragmenting their families just to pay for their overextended credit limits.

The demons' second line of attack was over-stimulating human minds with television, PCs, internet, radio, CDs, and VCRs. Even listening to and watching neutral material would crowd out the best—the still small voice—thus weakening the power of God's Holy Spirit in the humans' lives.

Next came the ambush of reading material—catalogs and mountains of junk mail, magazines, and newspapers. All kinds of promotional materials offering peace, prosperity, and power for a small fee.

The last assault would come from twisting the gift of the Sabbath to such an extent that even recreation would be excessive. Sporting events, cultural events, media events should leave humans exhausted and unprepared for living from their center. The evil angels were instructed to go so far as to infiltrate fellowship gatherings to incite humans to gossip about those who are absent. Demons would involve humans in so much small talk that they would leave gatherings troubled and unsettled, but wouldn't know why.

The devil went so far as to suggest that Christians be allowed to talk to others about God—to attempt to be a witness—but the evil angels should allow them to fill their lives with so many good causes that they wouldn't have time for the Source and would go through all the motions under their own strength, eventually sacrificing their relationships and their health.

The point of this story hit home as I looked around my house one day. The housework was undone, the calendar full, schoolwork was in various locations, and the family was crabby. Taking control of our situation, being good stewards, does not constrict the movement of God's Spirit. Taking control to clear the confusion, orchestrate the noise, harness the resources, and focus on the essentials actually allows more quiet for the voice of God to speak. Taking control allows space for the Spirit to freely flow and transform. As one of my friends once said, "When the devil can't make me bad, he makes me busy." So take control of your world to allow God the greater control in your life.

We can steward time well when we take the larger view found in the assurance of Psalm 31:15, "My times are in [God's] hands."

Our Own Circle of Life

Relationships are the bedrock of life. Wise women keep their intimate and important relationships healthy. Through expressions of love, concern, apology when necessary, and playful affection, wise women let the people in their lives know they are important and involved in a mutually caring relationship.

As I mentioned at the beginning of this chapter, three of the areas I was most concerned about when I thought something fatal might happen to my husband were my relationship with him, my relationship with my children, and my relationship with our community of friends. This incident gave me a gigantic wake-up call in an arena I was completely blowing in life.

My husband, who is a marriage and family therapist, teaches the premarital couples he works with the concept of the emotional bank account. We each need to be making positive deposits to the emotional bank accounts of people we love. These deposits consist of thoughtful words and deeds, acts of caring and companionship, and affirming the life of another person. At some point, through tragedy, difficult transitions, or sheer developmental changes, we are going to need the love and support of those around us. Having conscientiously made deposits to their emotional bank accounts, there is "currency" available to us when we need to make withdrawals in the form of needing comfort or assistance or being unavailable at some future point.

"THE LAUGHTER" TREASURE HUNT

How would you rate yourself as a wise woman, given your stewardship over the various resources we've just discussed? Use the following scale in responding to each statement:

5=always   4=often   3=sometimes   2=rarely   1=never

_____ 1. I understand what my "product" is in the various areas of my life, and I seek the best raw materials I can find to help me produce this product.

_____ 2. I keep good track of all the people in my household.

_____ 3. I manage my physical health well. I am not obsessed with my physical appearance, but I practice healthy habits to keep myself as strong as I can be to accomplish my tasks in life.

_____ 4. I do a regular check on the internal wardrobe of my character.

_____ 5. I think things through, not accepting what everyone else thinks about a topic. I question well, and I am open to being questioned myself.

_____ 6. I keep an eye on finances.

_____ 7. I keep my stuff in good order, and I am diligent to keep my possessions to a manageable amount. I regularly get rid of what I don't need.

_____ 8. I use my time well, with the understanding that God is ultimately in charge of all that is in time and all that is outside of time.

_____ 9. I make positive deposits into the emotional bank accounts of those I love.

The scale for this assessment is 9 to 45. The higher your score, the more in control you feel of your resources and the more assured you are that you and God are ready for anything. You are more prone to laugh at the days to come, unflustered by potential snares and potholes in the road.

An Issue of Contentment

Good stewardship is really a contentment issue. When we are content, we are not grasping for the next thing—the newer or bigger or neater thing. Fully embracing what has graciously been given to us, we are free to lovingly care for it and joyfully share it.

Everything in life that we have been given—whether it be time, talent, or treasure—is a gift from God. When we are content, we take better care of what we have. When we are free from our "wanting" mind, we can focus on the abundance already there and share it freely because we know we will always be cared for by our loving heavenly provider, whom we will never out give.

Are we content with how our children are (apart from the little rough edges that need sanding)? Do we genuinely enjoy the clothing we have? Are we amused and amazed by our own talents and gifts? Have we made peace with our household budget? Are we happy with ourselves and the precious corner of the world God has assigned to us to serve?

The Original Wise Woman's stewardship of her relationships yielded terrific benefits. One of the greatest blessings was the laughter she must have had with her family. Her children were vocal about their love for her (Proverbs 31:28). Her husband spoke glowingly and publicly about his esteem for her above all others (31:28-29). What made her such a treasure in their eyes? She was aware that she was God's gift to them and handled herself with generosity and effectiveness.

GOING DEEPER

Warm-up: Look at the Treasure Hunt in this chapter. What do you notice? What activities do you want to continue as a good steward? Where do you want to improve?

1. Review the five spiritual laws of God's economy and complete the chart below.

         The more you   the more you

       a.   a.

       b.   b.

       c.   c.

       d.   d.

       e.   e.

2. Ponder the following passage, drinking in every word. Let it penetrate your heart with the importance of each phrase. "God is able to make all grace abound to you, so that in all things at all times, having all that you need, you will abound in every good work" (2 Corinthians 9:8). What is God's measure of giving to us? What is the purpose of this generosity?

3. "The wise woman builds her house, but with her own hands the foolish one tears hers down" (Proverbs 14:1). Give examples of the different ways a wise woman builds her house. Give as many examples as you can of the various ways a foolish woman could tear her house down. How does this relate to good stewardship?

4. What are some ways we as wise women can practice good stewardship?

5. "The stewardship of our time is one of the most telling ways of measuring our trust." What does this mean? How does this tie in with "doing less but doing it with more passion, purpose, and power"?

6. As you read through the story of Satan and his angels, highlight or circle the ways you are tempted to misuse the resources and the life God has given you to enjoy and spend for Him. Look around your "house" and discern the ways chaos and clutter are effectively keeping you from a rich, full life in the Spirit. Make and share with others a plan for clearing away the chaos.

7. How will good stewardship help *you* laugh at the days to come?

Assignment for this week: Honestly and prayerfully ask the Holy Spirit to show you the chaotic or distracted places in your life. Remember that God works gently with those who are sincerely seeking. Ask for His guidance and wisdom in knowing how to become more focused on the gifts God has given you and how to use them to glorify and enjoy Him.

7

YOU ARE GOD'S GIFT TO OTHERS

Her children arise and call her blessed; her husband also, and he praises her: "Many women do noble things, but you surpass them all."

PROVERBS 31:28-29

Seek to be a first-rate version of you, rather than a second-rate version of someone else.

JUDY GARLAND

Have you ever compared yourself to someone else? How did you fare? How did the other person come out? The bad thing about comparisons is that someone always loses. If you perceive the other person to be better than you are, you lose. If you perceive yourself to have the advantage, the other person loses. Not only is esteem lost, but the opportunity to be an authentic peer with that person—to find out all the wonderful things God is doing in her life, to see what partnerships you could be forging—is lost.

You are deeply, passionately, and eternally loved by God. Not only does God love you, God also likes you! But still we sit in a Bible study or a women's fellowship, or we stand in line at the department store checkout or at a back-to-school ice cream social and compare ourselves with others. Being women, we most likely are not faring well in our comparisons, so we ask, "Why can't I be more like…?" "Why am I here?" "Was God just kidding when He put me here?"

If you've asked these questions, you are in very good company. A beautiful queen in Old Testament times wondered what she could do to help her people, the Jews. When Esther's uncle, Mordecai, asked her to go to the king so he would repeal the edict to murder the Jews, Esther essentially asked, "What can I do? The king hasn't asked me to come into his presence for thirty days. Anyone who approaches the king without being commanded to can be put to death!"

But Esther's wise uncle said, "Who knows whether you have not attained royalty for such a time as this?" (Esther 4:14 NASB).

After fasting for three days, and having the Jews in her city fast for three days, Esther approached the king, and he issued a decree that would save the Jews.

Like He did for Esther, God knows where you are now, and He has a purpose for you. You are the wife God sent to your spouse, the mother He sent to your children, the friend He sent to your friends, and the peer He sent to your colleagues. It is no mistake that you are who you are, and you are where you are at this point in history and on this planet!

Perfect Gifts

The perfect gift has three key elements.

First, the gift is well-timed. Many of the gifts I have given in my life are quilts I have made. A well-timed gift means the quilt I construct for a baby gets to the child before she enters college. Not really! Gifts have their maximum impact when they are given on the proper day—not too early and not too late.

Second, the gift takes into consideration the tastes and needs of the recipient, as well as the occasion for the gift. Several years ago, my dear friend Theresa had her second child. Within minutes it became obvious that the tiny boy was in severe distress. Within hours we knew that his heart was not functioning properly. Within a week he received a transplant of a tiny walnut-sized heart. To celebrate Sam's spirit and God's faithfulness, I chose a quilt block of pastel colored hearts set in primary-colored balloons. Members of our Bible study and moms' groups signed each quilt block with praises and continued prayers for Sam's health and growth. Theresa lets me borrow the quilt to take with me whenever I speak on gifts and share Sam's remarkable life. He has grown enough that he knows his life and his quilt are special in God's work. When God sent His great gift to us—Jesus!—He took into account our human nature, our sinfulness, and the Christ-shaped hole each of us has in our lives. God's gifts are perfectly designed.

Third, a gift should be so well-done that the creator or giver should be proud to put his or her name on it. I sign and date each quilt I make. There's also a famous basket-making mill in Ohio that has each weaver initial and date their creations. God's handwriting was all over Jesus.

One autumn Sunday morning, as I was making my rounds as director of Children's Ministries at the church I was serving, the three-year-olds were thick into the story of creation. They were sitting on the floor enraptured by the teacher who was recounting the days of creation. She said, "And on the fourth day, God created day and night." One sweet little cherub piped up, "Well, that was a good idea!" In the same way, I imagine God crossing His arms proudly over His chest after forming each of us and saying, "Now that was a good idea!"

Each one of us is a special creation—a gift from God. He created us to live in this specific time and place: "All the days ordained for me were written in your book before one of them came to be" (Psalm 139:16). Not only were we created for a specific time, but our existence is intricately woven into the world and into the lives of those around us. God uses us to meet the needs of people around us and to perform specific tasks: "We are God's workmanship, created in Christ Jesus to do good works, which God prepared in advance for us to do" (Ephesians 2:10). And just as God created Adam and Eve and "saw all that he had made and it was very good" (Genesis 1:31). He says the same thing about us—His handiwork. His signature is all over us.

When We Can't Hear the Music

But not all of us are ready, willing, or able to embrace and celebrate that we are God's gift to others. Dysfunctional parenting, our basic sin nature, physical flaws, unrealistic goals as portrayed in the media, and failed attempts to be something or someone we're not may have convinced us that we are not worthy, lovable, or useful to anyone. What happens when we experience this kind of setback?

I am a walker. Three times a week I like to get out for a vigorous walk while listening to some praise music I have found especially designed for striders. One early summer midmorning, I was out exercising at the height of my aerobic capacity and the strangest thing happened. The music started slowing and the singing got sluggish. Every walker's sadness had occurred. The batteries in my tape player were dying. My music was gone, my rhythm was gone, my guide was gone. I gave up and went home.

Each of us has internal music. This internal music, when it's playing fully and joyfully, tells us we are precious to God and necessary to this world. If our "batteries" run low, we won't be able to hear our God-given music, and we won't be able to be the gift God means us to be. We need to keep our batteries charged and our channels clear to hear God's music for us.

There are four ways we impact the world with the gift of who we are: time, truth, trust, and 'tude.

The Gift of Time

Time as a gift is assessed in two ways: time spent *with* and time spent *on*.

When you spend time *with* people, you let them know that you *love* them and you *like* them! We all need to know we are liked! Young children feel this quite keenly. My college room-mate Vicki told me of a time when she was very young and said to her mother, "Mommy, do you like me?"

"Why, yes, honey, you know I love you very much!"

"But Mommy, do you *like* me?"

"Honey, Daddy and I both love you!"

Finally, exasperated, she said, "But Mommy, do you *like* (foot stomp) me?"

At last her mother understood and said, "Of course, honey. I like you very much."

We'll look at three ways in particular to spend time with people, but there are hundreds to discover. That's up to your imagination, inspiration, and individual situation.

Prayer. Praying with someone else has the power to unlock the gates of heaven and shower you both with blessings. Jesus commented on the power of at least two in prayer: "Again, I tell you that if two of you on earth agree about anything you ask for, it will be done for you by my Father in heaven. For where two or three come together in my name, there am I with them" (Matthew 18:19-20).

One morning a dear friend came into my office to give me an update on some conditions in her life. Near the end of our brief time, I asked her if we could pray together. In the midst of our prayer, I welled up with gratitude for her and the use of her plentiful gifts in the ministry of our church. I was truly thankful for her life.

A couple days later a beautiful card came in the mail. It read, "Thank you so much for your friendship! You are such a blessing to me and my family. Talking and praying with you yesterday morning helped me in ways I can't even explain. Such peace you shared! I have never had anyone pray a prayer of thanks for *me*—it felt awesome! Thank you for taking the time to share God's grace."

Two things struck me about this card. First, it only took five minutes of time for us to have our conversation. The Holy Spirit is so present and eager to be involved, that His activity can be experienced in something that takes just moments. Second, in 30-plus years of living, my friend had never heard anyone pray a prayer of thanksgiving for her. Praying with people should be a regular part of everyday life as we invite God's presence into everything we do and are.

Touch. We need to spend time touching those we love. Studies show we need at least 13 hugs a day to stay healthy. When my husband conducts marriage retreats and premarital seminars, he encourages couples to take time each day for a 30-second hug and a 7-second kiss. We need to remember to physically reach out to our kids and friends so they know they are loved! Young children even learn to read better when they are sitting securely with someone they love. They feel secure enough to take their time in sounding out words and correcting mistakes. Touch makes a difference!

Occasions. Jesus knew the power of spending time with people at special events. He attended weddings, funerals, and dinner parties. When we gather together, we bond in a special way. The invitation to my fortieth birthday party read, "In celebration of God's grace and the gift of your friendship." I realized as I reflected on 40 years of living that I had been blessed with an abundance of friends and an amazing family. I wanted to rejoice! The evening was full of cake and coffee, the laughter of children, lots of hugging, and an occasional "remember Robin when" story. I will never forget the people who were there. Many brought lovely gifts, but their presence was the most memorable treasure to me. "The toys and the presents will soon fade away, but they'll never forget the gift of a day."[1]

On the other end of the occasion spectrum is the unforgettable gift you give when you spend time with someone who is grieving. At a particularly difficult funeral for a young man who left three children and a stunned widow, I stood in line with a lovely woman who confessed, "I just don't know what to say." Having been in pastoral ministry, I could assure her that our friend was in such a condition that she really did not hear the words we said, but keenly felt our presence and our hugs. When people are grieving they need to have genuine people around them offering authentic support and the necessary space and time to mourn and heal. There are times when words are elusive, but a heartfelt hug or a pat on the hand says what the most carefully crafted phrases cannot.

It is no small struggle to give this gift of time "with." It does require sacrifice and some careful planning to get everything done. But the benefits to both the giver and the recipient are evident in this wonderful poem by Brenda Clapp.

As I was folding laundry one day,
The telephone began to ring.
While I was talking on the phone I noticed
The dishwasher needed unloading.

So, as I started to unload the dishwasher
And talked on the phone
My five-year-old loudly requested
an ice cream cone.

As I served the ice cream
And finished my call,
I remembered I had a shower gift
To get at the mall.

I shuffled through the kitchen junk drawer
Now where is the coupon for that department store?
DING DONG! Someone was at my front door.

And now, ice cream all over my floor.
Be angry, sin not, I thought as I went to the door.
"Whoever said that," I mumbled, "hasn't seen this
messy floor."

"Ma'am, would you like to buy a candy bar
to support a good charity?"
"Of course, I'll get my purse,"
but finding it quickly would be a true rarity.

"Can you wait just a minute?"
I said to the boy.
My purse could be anywhere in the house,
My daughter thinks it's a toy.

I paid the young man and thought to myself,
Weird fashion these days, to wear pants so droopy.
Upon closing the front door, my two-year-old yelled,
"MOMMY, I'M POOPY."

I made my way up the cluttered stairs,
To find a clean diaper was my goal.
I tripped over a Barbie
And down the stairs it did roll.

For crying out loud! I thought to myself,
I think I've put that doll away twice!
"&%#$%," I said under my breath,
Such language, although said quietly, what a terrible
vice.

Forgive me, Lord, for the things I think and say.
I guess I'm a little harried today.
I promise to keep my frustration at bay.
Seeking your counsel always makes things okay.
I'll remember that next time my nerves start to fray.
Now…what did I come upstairs for, anyway?

During my short prayer
At the top of the stairs,

I spied my daughter's bedroom
All cluttered with dolls and stuffed bears.

"What a zoo!" I exclaimed
and began making the bed.
Suddenly, "Mommy, where are you?" I heard,
"What is it?" I said.

Then I saw her doing
Her dirty diaper dance.
Amidst praying and bed-making,
I'd forgotten to change her pants.

Is it bedtime yet? I wondered,
As I changed the dirty drawers.
I really do need to finish
All of these household chores.

I don't have much trouble starting the work,
That's true,
It's completing the task
That is so hard to do.

My daughter stood up
And gave me a great hug.
Her sloppy kisses always give
My heartstrings a tug.

I guess all this housework
Will just have to wait.
I want to play with my kids
Before it's too late.

"They grow up so fast,"
my mother would say.
"Before you know it, you'll be asking
for their attention someday."

We did puzzles, colored pictures
And played all afternoon.

Frankly, for the first time,
I thought bedtime came too soon.

After teeth brushing, book reading
And prayers were all said,
My kids were safely, soundly, happily
Tucked into bed.

I surveyed the unfolded laundry, dirty dishes
And sticky floor.
"How was your day?" my spouse asked,
As he came through the door.

"Oh, honey," I answered,
"You know how some days are,
the only thing I finished today,
was a chocolate candy bar."

Brenda's girls certainly benefited from her time *with* them. And she did, too. But we also spend time *on* people, as well. Often covert and unnoticed, there are three noteworthy ways to be this gift to others.

More prayer. Just as it was in spending time "with," at the top of the list of ways to spend time "on" people is prayer. When we spend time on people in prayer, we gift them in ways that are mysterious, powerful, and often known only to God. Although it may seem futile, unfruitful, and like shooting in the dark, uplifting people the Holy Spirit lays on your heart at seemingly odd times is cooperating with the Almighty in bringing His kingdom to earth. How often has God laid someone on your heart and when you mention it to them, they respond that they were indeed in need and were blessed to know you had thought of them?

Equally important is consistent, daily prayer for God to bless, teach, and guide the special people in your care. These fortunate, albeit often unknowing recipients of your constant efforts on their behalf may be children, parents, spouses, friends, or colleagues and neighbors for whom you are concerned.

Sometimes we run out of "material" when praying for these loved ones. After seven weeks of "Please bless Susie," we may long for meatier prayers that change the world because they change us and the people for whom we are praying. "The Bible is a great vehicle for focusing our communication with the Lord,"[2] says Cheri Fuller. Choosing Scripture passages to meditate on and translate for the people we love can be fun, rewarding, and bring surprising results. This practice aids our deeper understanding of the Word. It helps us stay alert for specific ways our prayers are being answered. Several terrific passages to consider for this practice are Colossians 1:9-14; 3:12-17; Ephesians 3:14-21; 16:10-18; and 1 Corinthians 9:10. You might even choose passages in Proverbs and pray particular wisdom to come into the lives of those you love! The key to this kind of prayer is to blanket the person in your requests and leave the details up to God.

Notes and cards. Which envelopes do you open first when shuffling through the mail? Is it the envelope marked "Resident," or the one with your name written on it? Do you eagerly dive into the package that promises to be a bill or a solicitation for yet another credit card? No. The first piece of mail that captures your attention is the hand-addressed, pretty envelope bearing the return address of someone you love. To read a nice wish from a friend or a lovely piece of news from a dear family member warms our hearts and brings smiles to our faces. Even if the note bears a poem or sentiment penned by another author, we know that a few days earlier someone spontaneously thought of us! Maybe they were standing in the store and grabbed a card for us. Perhaps they were having some quiet time and our name popped into their heads, and they knew they had to drop us a quick note. Maybe they saw something on television or heard a piece of music that they knew we would love. Whatever the circumstance, they not only thought of us, they took the time to write a thoughtful note that would touch our hearts.

One afternoon, my kids thought I had lost my mind when I sifted through the mail. I got excited and then cried within the span of five minutes. My precious friend Claudia had sent not one, but two special treats in an envelope! The first was a note handwritten on a simple card thanking me for our friendship and looking forward to our next time together over coffee. The second was a tiny little card with "Faith" etched into the sand of the seashore on the cover and a beautiful little quote inside. Claudia has 3 talented, active children, at least 14 pets, and a flourishing marriage to a gifted physician. She does not have a lot of discretionary time in her day. But without having any special reason except for her kind thoughtfulness, she took time to send me a heartfelt celebration of friendship. Claudia *is* a gift.

Just imagine how different your life would be if once each week you sent a heartfelt note to someone who means something to you. You would send out gifts of love and memory to special people in your life. And since "you reap what you sow," just imagine all the goodness that would come back your way. The most wonderful thing about giving this kind of gift is that it can be done by those who are housebound, it can be done in just a few moments in time, and it costs almost nothing.

Leave a legacy. A final way to spend time on people is to guard your reputation for the generations to come. In Chapter 4 I introduced a conversation I had with Dr. Jay Kesler at Taylor University. As he and I became acquainted, I introduced myself as a former Taylor student and friend of his youngest son. While I am certain he found that interesting, what brought the light of recognition to his eyes was realizing who my relatives were. "Oh, your grandfather is Loyal Ringenberg. He's one of my heroes. That must mean your uncle is Bill Ringenberg (a history professor on campus). So you are the daughter of Walt and Lenore Chernenko. We went to school together. Your father was a steady, stable man of God." How grateful I was that my ancestors had behaved themselves! It reminded me of Joshua 24:13: "So I gave you a land on which you did not toil and cities you did not build; and you live in them and eat from vineyards and olive groves that you did not plant." Those who had gone before me had paved the way for me to walk a well-lit path. Even if your relatives did not smooth the way for you, you can still see yourself as a gift in this way. Your godly, Christlike living is sowing fertile seeds for those in your family who are coming after you. Just be who you are as you watch God's plan unfold in your life and in the lives of your family.

Your preservation and retelling of your history are immeasurable gifts to those around you. My entire family, including grandparents and siblings, love poring over family albums that not only have pictures in them, but journaling and storytelling woven among the photographs. One of my children's favorite bedtime activities is snuggling on the couch under a quilt and playing "tell me a story about when I was a baby." They love hearing their own stories and delight in the retelling of funny and embarrassing antics. They find true pleasure and soul satisfaction in hearing tales of their tenderness and discovery. Give the generations the gift of their heritage—communal and individual.

The Gift of Truth

Chapter 4, "How to Have a Smart Mouth," had a great deal to say about telling the truth. As we look at the gift of truth you give to others, we focus on what it means for you to *be* the truth. While Jesus stated nearly eight times in the Gospels, "I tell you the truth," one of His most shocking and controversial claims is that He *was* the truth (John 14:6). Why was Jesus the truth? He completely and without hesitation understood and lived out His purpose. He was authentic; He was the earthly representation of His heavenly Father. He knew exactly what His music was and how to live it out each day.

Are you authentic in the way you live? Are you for real? Do you wear each day what you just love to wear or do you dress for the neighbors, the others in Bible study, or the mall walkers? Do your volunteer activities reflect heartfelt passions or are they social climbing maneuvers? Are your children involved in activities that are training them in the way they should go (Proverbs 22:6)? Or are they doing what the "in" crowd does so they (and you) won't be left out? Are you comfortable with your call and your identity as a deeply, passionately, eternally loved daughter of God? Or are you putting up a front to make people believe you are someone you hope to be or think you should be?

When we embrace the music God has gifted us with, when we let those patterns and notes God carefully crafted shine through our unique personality, we can move gleefully and confidently through our days. We will sleep peacefully, as well.

Hans Christian Andersen tells a remarkable story of three characters who impacted their community with the truth about the truth. In "The Emperor's New Clothes," we meet a royal clotheshorse who is so vain all he can think about is the next outfit he's going to parade in front of his loyal subjects. Two con men pass through the kingdom to offer their assistance in suiting his royal highness in threads that are so magnificent only the wise and informed can see them. They work for weeks, all the while inviting in the king's advisors to check on the progress. Not wanting to be genuine and tell the truth (and be labeled a fool), each advisor plunges the situation into deeper darkness by fussing over the nonexistent outfit.

Finally the day comes for the king to show his finery to the empire. The word has gone out to the subjects that this cloth is only visible to the "in" crowd. Everyone gets the message except for one little guy who can't read the memo. As the king is regally strutting through the streets of his dominion, this little genuine article blurts out rather loudly, "But he hasn't got anything on!" Little by little, a snicker ripples through the crowd, then some outright guffaws. Soon there are people doubled over with laughter in the gutters. As if the scene were not bizarre enough, the last line of the story says, "This made the emperor anxious for he knew they were right. But the emperor thought, 'I must keep up appearances through the procession.' And the emperor walked on still more majestically, and his aides walked behind him and carried his imaginary train, which didn't exist at all."[3]

Fear and deceit ruled the community when the truth was submerged. Glee and relief took over when the truth surfaced. The truth has a way of bonding people together. John 8:32 says, "You will know the truth, and the truth will set you free." Henry David Thoreau said, "Between whom there is a hearty truth, there is love."[4] There is love because nothing in all the world feels so good as being completely ourselves and feeling completely accepted. When you are in the presence of a truthful person you can relax. You leave your meeting with her saying, "I'm a better person for having been with her."

You are a gift to others when you are real. You give a gift to others when you teach and encourage them to be real.

The Gift of Trust

When you are honest with others, they know they can trust you. You are a remarkable and rare gift in this world when you are someone who can be trusted. Reflect on someone who has been true to you in heart, word, and action. These people are treasures to relax with because you know you are safe. You can share your fullest self, whatever attitude and disposition you have at any particular time.

But have you ever been betrayed, even in a tiny way? Perhaps someone shared something you said in confidence that you never meant others to hear. Maybe you were in a fun and growing friendship with someone when they seemed to suddenly change into someone else before your eyes. Maybe you invested a lot of time and energy into a younger person only to have her dump all of the good learning and growing she had done to follow an inferior path. Perhaps you were betrayed as a young person by someone who should have been watching out for, nurturing, and protecting you. Whenever we are betrayed, it hurts and we experience tremendous loss.

Even the psalmist lamented over being let down by those around him in whom he trusted. Hurt and shocked, he cried out to God, sometimes with a plea for revenge. An entire chapter of Proverbs is dedicated to the meaning of trustworthiness and the complete chaos that comes to life when someone we thought we could count on turns out to be untrustworthy.

Grace does indeed abound, and rebuilding broken trust is the subject of the entire book of Hosea. It is basic to the character of God to repair trust, to forgive, to redeem, and to restore. And the good news is that with a little common sense and uncommon wisdom, we can be women who won't need so much grace in this respect because we can be more trustworthy in the first place.

Being trustworthy is setting aside your own agenda or opinions and listening with the wisdom of Christ.

To be the gift of trust means we are very careful with our words. (See Chapter 4.) Not only will we not gossip and break confidence, we will know ourselves well enough to let our yes be yes and our no be no. When we say something, we can be trusted that it is exactly what we mean. One of my favorite examples of this is my editor at Harvest House. Barbara is a wise woman whom I deeply trust with my writing. She will tell me if something stinks or if it is sterling. She doesn't flatter, and she doesn't withhold genuine praise. She is a gift to me and to my writing career. Are you honest in your relationships? Do you allow others to be honest with you?

You are a gift of trust when people know that as far as you are able, you will be there for them. Your trusted presence may be in the form of prayer, actual physical proximity, or through

phone and email conversations. You become more trustworthy
in this respect when you also let people know up front if you
can't be there for them at a particular time. Several women
whom I went to for input on this book were very wise in saying
they really didn't have the time, at that point, to give me the
thoughtful participation they felt this situation warranted. In
their candor, they taught me two things about my ability to
trust them. First, they believe in what I'm about and wanted to
make quality contributions rather than simply chattering off
the cuff. So I know I can trust them to be thoughtful and thorough. Second, I know that when they say they can participate,
they will be telling me the truth.

You are trustworthy when you walk with people through
their testing times. Debbie highlights her relationship with one
such friend:

> A dear friend of mine has been a gift from God in
> my life over the past five years. I have an amazing
> amount of trust in her. She has been through
> many difficult times with me as a source of support
> and guidance. She was the "wise one" I went to
> during my first pregnancy. She was a great source
> of support during several challenging times in my
> personal life. She was the one there for me
> through difficulty at work. Next to my husband,
> she is probably the person I trust most in my life.

Being there for people is sometimes simply a matter of listening. We may, at times, be hesitant to be there for people
because we feel we don't have the answers. But as Kathy said,
"Being trustworthy is when a friend can set aside her own personal agenda or opinions and listen with the wisdom and compassion of Christ. When you can reveal the ugliness and hurt
within yourself to that friend, and she can help you identify the
sin causing the pain, together you can navigate the way back to
an obedient life in Christ." Kathy has known the joy of being this
kind of friend for others.

Linda echoes this experience in a tribute to someone who has given her the gift of trust. "My best friend is the most trustworthy soul I know. She allows me to say anything I need to, without judging me. She listens not only to my words, but also to my feelings. She allows me to vent. Being a wife and mother has been far more difficult than I ever imagined. My friend helps me by listening to my joys and frustrations. What I say to her is never discussed with others."

Susan speaks of her marriage as the most trustworthy relationship she has: "Each day my husband gives me a daily gift of trustworthiness. We actually give it to each other as we daily make the decision to love each other exclusively. Love is a daily, hourly, and sometimes a moment-to-moment decision. I do feel Darrell gives me this gift of trustworthiness each day, and for that I am blessed."

The gift of trust that you give simply by being present and consistent is a truly healing phenomenon. We can never overestimate the outcome for good that being trustworthy can bring. It may take time, but the results are powerful. One of my friends shared the benefits of one such relationship. "There was a time, about 12 years ago, when I was going through a deep depression. My mother had died, we were losing our business, and I felt my church had betrayed me. I was seeing a counselor who, in her infinite wisdom, felt that I also needed a spiritual advisor. It was only through the loving counsel of one of the ministers at church that I remained at my church, happy in my decision. He showed me true loyalty, unconditional love, and a path that I've remained on to this day. He gave me the gift of my own confidence that I had lost along with my faith—not in Jesus—but in my fellow Christians. Jesus is my true guide, but having the love and trust of my brothers and sisters in Christ is necessary in my faith walk."

Cheree has known the deep soul satisfaction of being God's wise woman, trusting that just by showing up she could make a difference with God's help. "I was a tremendous support to a friend in need through the short life of a very sick child. I found strength that I didn't know I had, and I was able to allow God to speak through me in times of incredible sorrow. I truly believe that God used me in those few months to show others what a personal relationship with Him can do."

The foundational characteristic of God in the Old Testament is wrapped up in one beautiful Hebrew word: *hesed. Hesed* means God's faithfulness, trustworthiness, and consistency to His people. Although not necessarily a popular virtue in our wild world today, faithfulness is the bedrock that keeps our culture from completely falling apart. Faithful spouses, faithful parents, faithful friends, children, and mentors are the unsung heroes that enable others to stay healthy and safe. You are a gift when you can be trusted.

The Gift of 'Tude

'Tude. You are an immeasurable gift to others in living godly attitudes yourself and then wisely instructing and encouraging others to do the same. It is a source of constant wonder and relief to observe how markedly our lives can be changed simply by altering our attitudes!

Your attitude itself is a gift to others. The manner in which you interact with them may touch them, encourage them, call them to accountability, or give them peace and refreshment when the going is tough. Your attitude can be a remarkable gift to others when you share it to such an extent that they pick it up and make it part of their own. As a bumper sticker says, "Attitude is contagious. Is yours worth catching?" Three positive and essential attitudes are humility, enthusiasm, and gratitude.

Jesus graciously and plainly reveals the attitude of humility, as described by St. Paul in Philippians 2:5-11:

> Your attitude should be the same as that of Christ Jesus: Who, being in very nature God, did not consider equality with God something to be grasped,

but made himself nothing, taking the very nature
of a servant, being made in human likeness. And
being found in appearance as a man, he humbled
himself and became obedient to death—even
death on a cross! Therefore God exalted him to
the highest place and gave him the name that is
above every name, that at the name of Jesus every
knee should bow, in heaven and on earth and
under the earth, and every tongue confess that
Jesus Christ is Lord, to the glory of God the Father.

In our house, if you are uppity or "high on your own stock," we
say you are a bit too "full of yourself." Jesus was not full of Himself in terms of thinking He was too good to do anything. He was
extremely full of His essence in that His very nature, His utter
core, is loving service. He was so full of Himself that He could
empty Himself of honor, aloofness, and power to show up on
earth to represent the nature of God to those in desperate need of
insight—us! Just when I'm feeling too good to make someone's
sandwich or listen to someone's problem, just when I don't have
time to wipe a tear because I have something else to do, just when
I don't want to be bothered with petty, selfish, and mean-spirited
people, I am reminded of Jesus' example of attitude. I realize how
blessed I am that He came to earth to be my role model and
guide. He provided food, listened to problems, comforted, sacri-
ficed, and dealt with ornerier people than I'll ever meet! And His
Spirit does the same for me each day of my walk with Him.

The second indispensable attitude is enthusiasm. If there is
one word that describes the Original Wise Woman it is enthusiasm! She is strong, respected, generous, industrious, worry-
free, and appropriately busy. She rolls up her sleeves to dig into
her day. She gathers, supports, encourages, and administers with
energy and purpose.

Enthusiasm is the direct outgrowth of inspiration. "Inspiration" literally means we are working "in spirit." When we are

overburdened by the details and minutia of life, when we don't really care about the project, when we are trying to fit a square peg into a round hole, when we have said yes when we really meant no, we are in danger of being frustrated and despondent over the tasks of life before us. When our vision is clouded by hurt, depression, or greed, enthusiasm cannot survive. True enthusiasm comes from walking hand in hand with God through the Holy Spirit, who keeps us on the paths of peace and pleasantness. True enthusiasm is born of authenticity, of doing what we know we are called to do and not being tempted to take on other roles or tasks to please or impress others. A wise woman in a wild world sticks to the basics, stays free of worldly attachments, and maintains divine connection with the guiding Spirit of God. Because of this, she can pursue her life with passion, knowing the true value of everything she does.

Last but not least, there are few greater gifts we can pass on to the next generation than that of teaching and modeling gratitude.

My Grandma Mary was a sweet, simple peasant from the Ukraine. She literally "came over on the boat" and worked out a life with her husband farming and raising eight children in Michigan. My father was her second son.

As is sometimes the case in families, we didn't see my father's side of the family very much, but I always knew my Grandma Mary was a woman of deep faith who was truly devoted to God. One profoundly special visit from Grandma came when my daughter, Madison, was about five, and my son, Grant, was one. I hadn't seen Grandma Mary in ten years, and my daughter had never met her at all! We decided to take Grandma to a concert one afternoon, so we all piled into our van with Grandma Mary and Madison sitting in the second row.

The conversation between them was engaging and charming. Madison was fascinated with a story of a pink flannel night-gown Grandma had received the Christmas before. Grandma described its warmth and softness, and she cooed over the fact that God had sent it to her at just the right time. She talked of how much she appreciated the gift, her warm and snuggly treasure.

I sat at the steering wheel feeling like a total jerk. I was at the height of my selfish entitlement period, and listening to her enthusiastic and genuine gratitude over a nightgown made my heart break for its hardness and melt for her authentic goodness.

Two weeks later we received the phone call that she had died in her sleep. She died just as she had lived, quietly and completely resting in God's grace.

Madison and I made the five-hour trip to Grandma's tiny Michigan hometown for her funeral. We talked on the way of Grandma's poverty, her many children, her pink flannel night-gown, and her love for God.

At the service, Madison asked for a few minutes alone at the open casket. I stood a respectful distance away, letting her have her space. I watched as her little lips formed a farewell to her great-grandmother. Then she blew a kiss and waved goodbye. As she stepped away, I moved in to meet her and asked her what she had said. Even at a young age, my wise daughter knew that some things are private. "That's not for me to talk about right now, Mommy."

On the way home, she asked, "Mommy, do you want to know what I said to Grandma Mary?"

"Well certainly, honey, if you want to tell me."

"I told her she and I would always be friends, and I would miss her very much."

My grandmother had given my daughter a gift in just one meeting. She had touched Madison's heart with her own warm gratitude. And she had helped me onto the road of recovery from the materialistic, possession-driven lifestyle by which I was being consumed. She embodied the utmost wisdom in Psalm 107:43, "Whoever is wise, let him consider the great love of the Lord."

"I AM A GIFT" TREASURE HUNT

Use the following scale in responding to each statement:

5=always 4=often 3=sometimes 2=rarely 1=never

_____ 1. I spend time with people praying about things that are causing them concern.

_____ 2. I spend time giving and receiving affection and affirmation through touch.

_____ 3. I make it a priority to be with people, marking important transitions and milestones with them.

_____ 4. I spend time on people by praying for them.

_____ 5. I send notes and cards for special occasions or "just because."

_____ 6. I seek to leave a positive legacy for my family by building a good reputation.

_____ 7. I seek to leave a legacy by preserving memories in the form of things I can pass on to my family.

_____ 8. I live truthfully so people around me don't have to wonder about my motives, attitudes, personality, or beliefs.

_____ 9. I live in a manner that promotes trust in those around me.

_____ 10. I exhibit genuine humility.

_____ 11. I exhibit authentic enthusiasm.

_____ 12. I exhibit gratitude.

You can score between 12 and 60 points on this Treasure Hunt. The higher your score, the more likely people experience you as the gift you were meant to be to this world. In what ways can you become more of God's gift to others?

It's Good to Be the Gift

Box up comparisons and put them on the shelf. They are not the packages God intends for you to open. They don't even enter the mind of the woman who is so busy being wise she has no time for self-defeating mischief. There has never been, is not now, and never will be another person just like you. You *are* God's gift for others! If you long to build solid relationships with colleagues, friends, family members, and people in your community, you will make the greatest strides by embracing your unique giftedness in this world and living joyfully in the patterns, fabric, and music God has designed for you.

GOING DEEPER

Warm-up: Biblically, the word "blessed" means "happy." When we read "her children will call her blessed," we hope someday our families and friends will bless us or appreciate us for what we have done in their lives. What if this "blessed" actually means our family and friends will remember us as happy, peaceful, fulfilled people? Does this change the way you approach your days?

1. In what ways are you God's gift to others?

2. What are the three elements of a perfect gift?

    a.

    b.

    c.

3. Consider Mordecai's question to Esther: "Who knows but that you have come to royal position for such a time as this?" (Esther 4:14b). What do you perceive to be one or two tasks you have been given by God to do?

4. Four ways we impact the world with the gift of ourselves are through time, truth, trust, and 'tude. Give some examples of people who have been gifts to you and what they did.

5. What are some of your favorite ways to spend time *with* others? What would you like to start including or doing more of?

6. What are some of your favorite ways to spend time *on* others? What would you like to start including or doing more of?

7. In what situations do you need to act as the truthful child in "The Emperor's New Clothes"?

8. Describe a time someone has been "truth" with you and how it impacted your perception of yourself. Make a note of someone you would like to be more authentic with and how you would like it to impact your relationship.

9. The three 'tudes we covered are humility, enthusiasm, and gratitude. Offer some other positive attitudes that you have seen in other people that have made an impression on you. How did those attitudes affect you?

Assignment for this week: Pick one of the gifts (time, truth, trust, 'tude), and live it to the fullest each day!

GOD'S PRICE IS RIGHT

I know that everything God does will endure forever; nothing can be added to it and nothing taken from it.

ECCLESIASTES 3:14

A love affair with knowledge will never end in heartbreak.

MICHAEL GARRETT MARINO

Since 1956, contestants have been responding to the invitation "Come on down!" issued by television's longest running game show in history, *The Price Is Right*. Why is it so much fun to play and watch? Contestants love matching wits with the various games that promise big prizes if they make the right assessments about the value of specific items. Viewers get a charge out of the sheer emotion displayed by players when they estimate correctly and win the prizes. Host Bob Barker says, "I like to see everyone win. It's more fun for me."[1]

Max Lucado tells a story of two department store vandals who entered the store at night with great mischief on their minds. They didn't steal any merchandise, they simply switched the price tags on everything! If that weren't bizarre enough, the next day the store opened for business, and nobody even realized the prank for four hours. Lucado uses the story to make this unfortunate point: We switch the price tags in God's world all the time!

In God's great game of "The Price Is Right," God's assessment of worth is always right. The wise woman in a wild world has placed her values in God's economy. She knows the inestimable importance of getting back to the basics and the rich returns of staying on her path. As she invests in wise speech, she reaps the benefits of spending her words judiciously. Knowing that the God of all abundance has graced her with all she has, out of gratitude she cares for and utilizes all of these gifts with energy and prudence. Because God places the highest value on His human creation, she keeps her life simply occupied in acts of service to all around her any place and any time. As part of her stewardship, and in special acts of service, she spends the gift of herself in lavish and loving ways on the people closest to her. Finally, she knows that God has placed supreme value on her as His beloved child. She keeps Him first and lets Him lead.

You are deeply, passionately, and eternally loved by God.

I hope you can see this woman portrayed in the poetry of Proverbs 31 as a springboard for looking at characteristics all of us can cultivate, no matter where we are in life. Living is more about what we are than what we do. It is more about a life devoted to God, than a life wasted in comparisons, selfish ambition, and disorder. Successful, joyous living has to do with experiencing the everyday elements of our life and using uncommon wisdom in a wild world.

Most of all, *your* life has to do with the inescapable fact that you are deeply, passionately, and eternally loved by God. What He desires for you more than anything is a deeper, fuller, wider, and more robust understanding of His gracious intentions toward and through you. My prayer is that as you comprehend this more thoroughly and as your life is transformed, you will continue to accept Wisdom's invitation to walk and talk with her, learn from her, and change your world with her at your side. "Say to wisdom, 'You are my sister,' and call understanding your kinsman" (Proverbs 7:4).

After all, the Original Wise Woman—the woman of wisdom after God's own heart—is you.

GOING DEEPER

1. What price tags in God's economy have you switched? What steps are you taking to get them back in the proper order?

2. Have you finished your acrostic poem that was part of Going Deeper for Chapter 2? What did you learn about yourself? What did you learn about our loving God who uniquely created you?

3. Review the Treasure Hunts. Which ones most influenced your growth as a wise woman in a wild world?

4. Which wise woman characteristic was easy for you to grasp? Which still seems elusive?

5. As you reflect on the scripture used in this book, which passages have been most influential? How have you witnessed the Holy Spirit working through scripture in your life to bring about transformation?

6. How has your life been transformed through your study? What changes have taken place?

7. What do you believe your next step to be in your life with God?

LEADING
A STUDY GROUP

1. The "leader" should be the person who keeps discussion moving. She does not need particular biblical knowledge or skill. She should have read the chapter in the book and the scripture ahead of time to make herself familiar with the material.

2. Allow at least two hours for each discussion. Good discussion includes times of thoughtful silence. If you are done before two hours is up, do not feel compelled to stay in your seats for 120 minutes. Let the Holy Spirit guide your time together.

3. Keep a box of colored pencils, markers, or crayons close to your discussion area. Have note cards ready for people to write to wise women in their lives.

4. As your group feels led, begin each time with a recap of the previous week's assignment and how implementing it impacted your life.

5. Some groups like to begin and end in prayer. Some take prayer requests and keep a journal of God's hand moving through situations and lives. Follow whatever pattern is most growth-producing in your group. Now may be the time to talk through those patterns to discern if they indeed are the ones your group wants to continue. Be bold in trying something new!

NOTES

Chapter 1—The Wisdom Wingding

1. Os Guinness, *The Call* (Nashville: Word Publishing, 1998), p. 141.

2. Melissa Jansen, *Are You Kidding, God? Me, a Prudent Woman?* (Anderson, IN: Warner Press, 1998), p. iii.

3. Annie Chapman, "Why the Proverbs 31 Woman Drives Me Crazy," *Today's Christian Woman*, May/June 1992, p. 63.

Chapter 2—The Bottom Line

1. Cheri Fuller, *When Mothers Pray* (Sisters, OR: Multnomah Publishers, Inc., 1997), p. 30.

2. Anne Broyles, *Journaling: A Spiritual Journey* (Nashville: Upper Room Books, 1999), p. 11.

Chapter 4—How to Have a Smart Mouth

1. Penelope Stokes, *Simple Words of Wisdom* (Nashville: Thomas Nelson, Inc., 1998), p. 85.

2. Les and Leslie Parrott, *Like a Kiss on the Lips* (Grand Rapids, MI: Zondervan Publishing House, 1997), p. 28.

Chapter 5—The Service Advantage

1. Penelope Stokes, *Simple Words of Wisdom* (Nashville: Thomas Nelson, Inc., 1998), p. 109.

Chapter 6—Wise Laughter

1. Patsy Clairmont, "Not Her Again," *Focus on the Family,* September 1999, p. 3.

Chapter 7—You Are God's Gift to Others

1. Author unknown, cited in Laurie Beth Jones, *Jesus in Blue Jeans: A Practical Guide to Everyday Spirituality* (New York: Hyperion, 1997), p. 282.

2. Cheri Fuller, *When Mothers Pray* (Sisters, OR: Multnomah Publishers, Inc., 1997), p. 33.

3. William King, *Hans Christian Andersen's Fairy Tales* (Philadelphia, PA: Running Press, 1996), p. 15.

4. Henry David Thoreau, cited in Phillips, *Phillips' Book of Great Thoughts and Funny Sayings* (Wheaton, IL: Tyndale House Publishers, Inc., 1993), p. 317.

God's Price Is Right

1. Michael A. Lipton, "Bio," *People Magazine*, September 6, 1999, p. 149.

Mom Overboard

Robin Chaddock

Sink or swim. Is that the decision facing you? Caught in nonstop activities for your kids and bombarded by myriad choices, are you struggling and feeling like you're drowning every day?

Life counselor, personal coach, and busy mom Robin Chaddock offers 12 "Lifesavers" that will help you stay afloat and manage your life. These include:

- exploring your "divine assignment"—your God-given purpose
- dealing with the joys and difficulties of child-rearing
- creating stronger relationships
- discerning when to say yes and when to say no
- learning how to listen and how to be heard

Robin also helps you understand how each Lifesaver connects you to the true source of wisdom and strength—Jesus Christ.

Other Good Harvest House Reading

REMARKABLE WOMEN OF GOD
Elizabeth George

In this inspiring look at the lives of women in the Bible, best-selling author Elizabeth George reveals refreshing models of faith for today. Stories about Eve, Sarah, Mary, and other women from Scripture offer testimonies of changed lives and reflections on the remarkable strengths God cultivates in women who love Him.

RADICALLY OBEDIENT, RADICALLY BLESSED
Lysa TerKeurst

Lysa shares illustrations from her life along with inspiring, biblical insights as she describes what it means to be totally, unapologetically obedient to Christ.

A MARRIAGE WITHOUT REGRETS
Kay Arthur

Kay shares the principles for successful marriages found in the ultimate marriage handbook—the Bible. Speaking candidly about her failed first marriage, her conversion to Christianity, and her longtime marriage to Jack, Kay offers practical advice on effective communication, security and significance, difficult marriages, parenting, and God's guidelines for divorce and remarriage.

SASSY, SINGLE, AND SATISFIED
Michelle McKinney Hammond

This user-friendly devotional helps individuals searching to understand their place in the world draw closer to the true Lover of their soul. Bestselling author Michelle McKinney Hammond combines usuable scriptural principles for daily living with inspirational stories, quotes, and personal experiences of life, love, and men.

WHEN GOD PURSUES A WOMAN'S HEART
Cindi McMenamin

Within the heart of every woman is the desire to be pursued, cherished, and loved. *When God Pursues a Woman's Heart* invites women on a personal journey of discovery that looks at the many ways God loves them, and how He shows that love.

HARVEST HOUSE
PUBLISHERS